SAI BABA AND SAI YOGA

Indra Devi

PUBLISHING

© Indra Devi

All rights reserved. No part of this publication may be reproduced or transmitted in any form or by any means, electronic or mechanical, including photocopy, without permission in writing from the publisher. Reviewers may quote brief passages.

Indian Edition, 1999
ISBN-81-86822-64-X

Published & Distributed by:
Sai Towers Publishing
(A Unit of Sri Sathya Sai Towers Hotels Pvt Ltd.)
No. 23/1142, Vijayalakshmi Colony,
Kadugodi, Bangalore-560 067
INDIA
Tel   : 91 80 8451648
Fax   : 91 80 8451649
EMail : saitower@vsnl.com

Printed by:
D. K. Fine Arts Press Pvt. Ltd.
New Delhi - 110 052

SAI BABA

I went down to the sea,
where the breeze gently plays
with the waves.
Silver sands
and black rocks.
Lying still, I listened to their sigh
and heard
Sri Sathya Sai... Sri Sathya Sai... Sri Sathya Sai...

I went out to the fields
where the flowers awake
at daybreak.
Gay butterflies
and free birds.
Sitting still I listened to their cry
and heard
Sri Sathya Sai... Sri Sathya Sai... Sri Sathya Sai...

I went to to the mountains
where enchanted trees sleep
sound and deep.
Immense silence,
intense peace.
Standing still I looked to the sky
and heard
Sri Sathya Sai... Sri Sathya Sai... Sri Sathya Sai...

— **Indra Devi**

This book, like everything else in my life, is dedicated to

BHAGAWAN SRI SATHYA SAI BABA

I would like to express my grateful thanks to my friends and students who have typed and retyped the manuscript of this book as it underwent many changes.

Glennys Scibird, Erica Moore, June Summers, Lynn Poulton, Cora Grocott, Enakshi Bhavnani, Indira Talwar, Elizabeth Palmer, Douglas and Marybeth Mahr, The Office of the Maharaja of Sandur, The Office of Mr. R.R. Kamani, The Office of Mr. Badami, Dr. Duane Robinson, Kathy van Dyke.

INTRODUCTION

This work has bloomed by the profound influence that Sri Sathya Sai Baba has had on Mataji Indra Devi since she met him in 1966. At present, Mataji is 99 years old and lives in Buenos Aires, Argentina, where she has founded a non-profit Yoga Institution named after her. She teaches Sai Yoga - a special yoga that reorients the traditional Hatha Yoga on spirituality.

All these years, large numbers of students have approached her to be enlightened by the insight she developed and experiences she had living intensely close to Bhagawan. Indra Devi has been one of Baba's most famous messenger to announce Him as a mighty source of Knowledge and Spiritual Power in almost eleven Latin American countries.

The current edition of this book has been revised and updated to meet the needs of the new millennium. As a close follower of this grand Dame of Yoga, we hope that this book will help to awaken readers to the spiritual wealth that rests in their hearts.

May Light, Peace and Love be always present in our ways.

PREFACE

Sai Yoga... "And what is that?" You may rightly wonder because you have never heard of it before. But then, neither had I, nor anyone else, for that matter.

A few years ago when I was conducting a class during our annual Teacher's Course in Tecate[1], and the students were about to assume the *yoga mudra*[2], I found myself telling them what they should be experiencing while assuming and maintaining this posture. I cannot say how or where the words came from, but they seemed to flow of their own volition, and I had only to voice them. When I had finished, the class sat still, spellbound.

"Mataji,[3] we have never experienced anything like this. What is it?"

"Sai Yoga," I answered without hesitation, surprising even myself with this explanation.

"Did Sai Baba teach it to you? When?"

"Right now, this very moment."

Since the class was already in its third week, all the students had, by then, heard from me a great deal about Sai Baba, and were, therefore, not too surprised. They knew that in India He was worshipped by millions as an *Avatar* (Divine Incarnation) and that He could perform any kind of miracle, from curing the sick and the blind, to producing, from seemingly nowhere, anything He wished to give His devotees.

And so it was, miraculously, that Sai Yoga was brought into being. Its practice involves not only physical and mental, but moral and spiritual aspects as well. It is primarily designed to produce a contemplative and meditative attitude of mind while performing the *asanas* (yoga postures) without diminishing or interfering with their beneficial effects upon the body. On the contrary, these become augmented. It results in a kind of complete self-analysis, and, consequently, self-transformation.

This new approach, which is likely to give a deeper insight into the inner being, is what makes the difference between the way in which the *asanas* are usually performed, and Sai Yoga, where the postures serve as stepping stones to the higher stages of Yoga, namely, the spiritual awakening. When you start practising them the way they are described later in this book, you will yourself become aware of the difference. But before going into a description of its practice, I must tell you how I happened to meet Sai Baba.

End Notes:
1. A small town in Mexico on the border of California, where Rancho Cuchuma, now the home of the Sai Yoga School, is located.
2. A squatting posture with both feet under the buttocks, and the spine and head erect. Illustrated on page
3. Mata: Mother in Sanskrit; *ji* is added as a sign of respect.

CONTENTS

Introduction
Preface

SAI BABA

1. How I Met Sai Baba — 1
2. My Second Trip to Prasanthi Nilayam — 14
3. Miraculous Experiences — 29
4. My Third Trip to See Baba — 32
5. Baba Calls Me Again — 39
6. More Miracles — 53
7. Baba's Birthday — 61
8. Baba is With Me All the Time — 67
9. Baba's Grace: For Husband and Mother — 70

SAI YOGA

10. Introduction — 73
11. The Cobra Posture — *Bhujangasana* — 81
12. The Forward Bend — *Paschimotanasana* — 85
13. The Twist Posture — *Ardha-Matsyendrasana* — 88
14. The Pelvic Posture — *Vajrasana* — 93
15. The Supine Pelvic Posture — *Supta Vajrasana* — 95
16. The Reverse Posture — *Viparita Karani Mudra* — 97
17. The Shoulderstand — *Sarvangasana* — 99
18. The Plough Posture — *Halasana* — 102
19. The Lotus Posture — *Padmasana* — 105
20. The Fish Posture — *Matsyasana* — 110
21. The Symbol of Yoga — *Yoga Mudra* — 112
22. The Headstand — *Shirshasana* — 116
23. The Sun Salutation — *Surya Namaskar* — 123

SAI
BABA

HOW I MET SAI BABA

In 1966, before I had even heard of Baba, a psychic in Los Angeles, Clara Schuff, had told me that I would soon be going to India, where I would meet an extraordinary Swami who was super human. Although at that time I had no plans whatsoever of going to India, nevertheless, two months later, I was on my way to Saigon and stopped over in India. I began to conduct meditations in Delhi at various temples and spiritual centres. From Delhi I went to Bombay, where the response was even more enthusiastic, probably because I was still remembered in that city. I had lived there for twelve years (from 1927 to 1939) first as a visitor, then as the wife of a foreign diplomat, and finally as a student of Yoga.

Before leaving for Saigon, I flew to Madras to see my old friend, Dr. Sivakamu, staying at the Theosophical Society in Adyar. There I met the Australian writer, Howard Murphet[1], and his charming wife, Iris, who knew of me through my books. Our conversation centered on various spiritual leaders in India and their work. In conclusion, Mr. Murphet said, "But of course, the greatest of them all is Sai Baba."

"Who?" I asked.

"Sai Baba. Sathya Sai Baba, the reincarnation of the great saint, the Sai Baba of Shirdi. Surely you have heard of Him!"

But I hadn't. Surprised at this, the couple tried to fill in the gaps in my knowledge about their Master.

"He is the brightest star in the spiritual firmament of India today. He is an *Avatar*, a Divine Incarnation."

"There is no one like Him," seconded Iris. "You must... you simply must meet Him."

Their enthusiasm, however, had a contrary effect upon me. The more they told me about their Swami and His miracles, the less I felt like meeting Him, especially after seeing His picture stuck on a wall of their room. It was a colour print clipped from a newspaper showing a fat, fierce-looking man in a bright orange robe, with a thick mop of black hair.

"Why this wild hairdo?" was all I could say, thinking to myself that if this was their Sai Baba, I didn't want to meet Him.

To convince me of His Divine powers, Mr. Murphet showed me a ring, which his Guru had supposedly materialised out of thin air.

"Swami always gives something to those He calls in for an interview. But He does not accept any money or gifts in return."

This was surprising because most gurus, swamis and teachers, with some exceptions, of course, have become very money conscious and greedy, even in India. The Murphets also told me that the old saint, Sai Baba of Shirdi, had told a few of his devotees, before passing away in 1918, that he would be back in human form eight years later. Accordingly, in 1926, little Sathya (full name Sathyanarayana Raju) was born in Puttaparthi, a small remote South Indian village. His birth was heralded by midnight twangs of the big *tambura* on the wall and the rhythmic beating of the *maddala* (drum) which scared everyone in the family beyond measure. They thought that ghosts must have been at play.

The many strange things that happened during Sathya's childhood caused His father to believe that He was possessed by spirits. To drive them out, he took the boy on pilgrimages, to priests, medicine men and even to an exorcist, in the hope that the child would become 'normal' like his brothers and sisters. But instead of getting 'better' he got progressively 'worse' as far as his parents were concerned.

On one occasion, for instance, the family took Him to the famous Veerupaksha temple in Hampi. At the time when *arati* (offering of the light by waving a camphor flame before the deity) was done, they suddenly saw their son standing on the altar in front of the *lingam*.[3] The infuriated father left the shrine only to see his Sathya standing quietly under a tree in the temple yard where he had left Him.

About a year later, the old man, on returning home, found his fourteen year old son distributing flowers, fruit and balls of sweet rice – which he was taking from the air by a mere wave of His hand – to members of the family and neighbours. The crowd around Him suggested to the parent that he acknowledge his son's Divinity. This angered the father to such an extent that he raised his cane to give the lad a beating for He was going too far and had to be stopped.

"Who are you," he shouted, "a ghost, a mad man or God?"

"I am Sai Baba[4]," answered the boy calmly, to everyone's surprise, for no one around knew who Sai Baba was.

Soon after, Baba left His home, declaring that He was no longer a member of their family and could not stay there. He said His *bhaktas* (devotees) were calling Him and that His work was waiting. Thus, at the age of fourteen (He was born on 23 November 1926) He proclaimed Himself as Sai Baba announcing that He had come to restore *Dharma* (righteousness), to uphold Faith, to establish the reign of Love, Truth and Peace, to bring people to the realisation of their spiritual origin, and to protect, guide and help His devotees.

"And that is what He has been doing ever since," added Howard. "Thousands upon thousands make their pilgrimage to His Ashram, Prasanthi Nilayam (Abode of Supreme Peace), in Puttaparthi to have His *Darshan*[5] or to receive His blessings, to ask for His help or to be guided or comforted by Him. He can multiply food, cure any disease, and even resurrect the dead.

He can also produce *vibhuti* (sacred ash), and articles of gold, silver and precious stones, besides clothing or anything else for presentation to his devotees."

"But if His message to the world is a spiritual one, why does He perform these kinds of miracles?"

"Didn't Christ do the same?" Iris asked, silencing me by this question.

In spite of all these wondrous stories, and the Murphets insistence that I wait for a few days for the arrival of Sai Baba in Madras, to the disappointment of my friends, I left for Vietnam.

"If it is my fate to meet Him, it will happen anyway," I told them. In Saigon, where I was staying with the then Indian Consul-General, Prince Pradymna Sinhji of Kotda-Sangani, I had the opportunity of seeing many Indians, most of whom revered Sai Baba as a living deity, an *Avatar*, a God in human form. There was, however, one exception: one man who called Him a fraud. "Do you believe anyone can really perform miracles nowadays? It's all magic tricks," he assured me. "Sai Baba wears a wig in which He hides the things and then gives them out to His followers."

This didn't seem plausible to me, especially since I had seen a brass statue of Sri Krishna produced by Baba, besides a silver ring He had materialised for Howard, and a golden medallion for his friend, Mr. Venkateshwara Rao, a mica magnate from Madras. It wasn't possible that such articles could be concealed in a wig, much less *vibhuti* which He gave to many people.

"Moreover," I argued, "a magician doesn't ever give away his rabbits, because then there would be no show the next evening. Besides, I was told that Baba doesn't accept any money or personal gifts, so how would he get all the costly objects He so often gives to His devotees?" Not receiving a reply, I finally asked the man, "Did you ever see Sai Baba?"

"No."

This took me by surprise. How could a person be so firm in making his accusations without having had any personal experience or knowledge? Incidentally, later on I came across quite a number of people who did not hesitate to disparage Sai Baba, just because someone told them something which they, in turn, had heard from a third party.

Slowly the desire to meet Baba began to grow. It was almost like a pull, a call, which became so strong that I went back to India, and, armed with letters of introduction from the Murphets, left Adyar for Puttaparthi.

On the way to Prasanthi Nilayam, we met another taxi carrying Dr. Sen. who was then Vice-Chancellor of Jadavpur University and later became Minister of Education, and Mr. Banerji of the Bangalore Science Institute. The cars stopped, and after exchanging greetings and introducing ourselves, Dr. Sen began sniffing the air and asked if I could smell the fragrance of jasmine around us.

"Baba must be with us," he remarked.

"Have you ever been to Puttaparthi before?" asked Mr. Banerji.

"No, this is my first visit, and I am returning tomorrow morning."

"You may never want to leave the place!" he remarked.

"But you are doing so and I shall have to do the same." We got into our cars after joining our palms in greeting, Indian style.

"*Namaste*," I said.

"Sai Ram," they replied.

When they drove away, it occurred to me that the fragrance which both of them had detected could have been that of the *patchouli* oil I usually use and, therefore, had nothing whatsoever to do with Sai Baba.

After driving for another four hours, we arrived in Puttaparthi and entered the grounds of Sai Baba's Ashram, Prasanthi Nilayam. I didn't know where to go, since there was no office, information counter, or anything of that kind. Luckily, a young Swiss school teacher, Gabriela Steyer, to whom I had a letter of introduction from the Murphets, came to my rescue and arranged a room for me in the main guest house where she was staying. On the veranda hung a framed list of rules and regulations. The first one read that no gifts of any kind, not even fruit or flowers (the customary offerings to a holy man), should be offered to Swami. Another rule suggested the wearing of clean and decent clothing. As I always wear a sari, even outside India, I was not concerned about decency when sitting cross-legged on the ground, which is difficult, if not impossible, in a short, narrow skirt.

My Swiss chaperon took me around to show me the hospital, where many supposedly hopeless cases had been cured by Baba — free of charge, of course. From there we went to the *Veda-Shastra* School[6] where boys are instructed in the wisdom of the ancient scriptures. Baba provides for their tuition, food, lodging and clothing. We also visited the press where *Sanathana Sarathi*, the monthly bulletin of the ashram, is published in Telugu and English. The other buildings were quarters for the five hundred or so residents of the Ashram, as well as a post office, bank, police station and a cafeteria run by volunteers. For a small sum one could buy a whole Indian meal in the cafeteria. Most of Baba's photographs which hung in all these places were obviously taken some time ago. "Now He is big and fat," I thought to myself, remembering the picture at the Murphets.

Back in my room, Miss Steyer began relating the many wondrous deeds she had been witnessing. The one that fascinated me was her account of how, on a holiday, Baba took all the ashramites to the river outside the village, and, after making a drawing with His fingers on the sand, took out a silver idol, then a chalice and finally a large spoon.

"He then filled the chalice with *amrita* (ambrosia or nectar) by squeezing it out of His clenched fist. He proceeded to give the fragrant nectar to each one of us, pouring it into our cupped palms," went on Gabriela. "When my turn came, I could see that the chalice was almost empty, but Baba simply tapped it with His fingertips and it became full again. Each one received a spoonful, although there were about five hundred of us, and the chalice could hold barely more that fifty spoonfuls."

I thought to myself that I would like to see this more than anything else, little suspecting that, in times to come, I would be witnessing many other unbelievable miracles.

Finally, she took me to the temple where Sai Baba was giving interviews. Soon a side door opened, letting out some people. I could hardly believe my eyes at the sight of a small, slender figure, clad in an orange robe, who appeared last. The handsome face with clean cut features had no resemblance whatsoever to the picture I had seen at the Murphets, except for the hair forming a sort of a black halo around His head. He looked so gentle, so compassionate, so human, and yet there was something about Him that set Him apart from everybody else. Saying a few words in Telugu (I speak only Hindustani) He disappeared behind the door. Someone translated: "No more interviews, it is too late." However, a few minutes later He appeared on the balcony upstairs and looked at the crowd down below. Our eyes met for a few seconds, and I felt certain that He was going to call me.

Suddenly my heart began pounding wildly. Moments later, I saw Baba standing in front of me, beckoning me to enter the interview room. As I stood up, I felt a strange sensation of continuing to rise, as if I was growing taller and taller, almost like leaving the ground. The sensation was very real. I felt Gabriela touch me and I opened my eyes; Sai Baba was now actually standing in front of me and beckoning me into the interview room. I could not feel the ground under my feet, and would have fallen down if Gabriela and a few other girls, who were also called in, had not held me up. I had experienced this sensation of leaving my body before, usually during meditation. Sai Baba sat down opposite me on the floor beside the armchair.

"I don't know why I am here," I began. "I don't want anything from You. In fact, I had not even heard of You before meeting the Murphets a few weeks ago. It was in Saigon that suddenly I was overcome by a desire to see You. The pull became so strong that I had to come here, although I was already on my way home."

"Where is home?" He asked.

"In Tecate, Mexico. Our ranch is on the border of Tecate, California, in the U.S.A." To make it clearer I pulled out from my handbag some snapshots of Rancho Cuchuma.

"You must come there, Swamiji; it is a beautiful place."

Taking my hand, he tapped my palm thrice saying, "I promise, I promise, I promise. I have said it three times and I shall keep my promise."

While looking at the photoholder, He saw Swami Vivekananda's picture and raised His eyes at me questioningly. I explained that, according to two clairvoyants, he was my protector and guardian angel. I added that I had asked for a sign to be given to me in the form of this picture if this were true. In 1957, I was in Delhi addressing the World Religions Conference. A man from the crowd came up to me, presented me with this photo of Swamiji and then disappeared. This convinced me that Swami Vivekananda wanted me to fulfil a certain mission which he had no chance to carry out in his last incarnation.

"He must have guided my steps to you, Swamiji," I said as I finished my story.

"You would not be here otherwise," Sai Baba affirmed. It seems that the Murphets were right, there was much more to Him than I had anticipated. Who is He really, I began to wonder.

"I am yours," startingly came the answer to my thoughts. "I reside on the altar of your heart. I shall never forsake you."

At parting He asked, "What do you want?" I had been prepared for this question by the Murphets and Gabriela, and I answered unhesitatingly.

"*Jyoti*... Light. Light in my heart."

"You have it."

"Not enough."

"*Bangaru, bangaru*[7]," He repeated with such loving tenderness in His voice that I melted. "I shall give you something to keep with you at meditation time." Saying this, He turned His palm downwards and made several fast circling movements in the air. Opening His upturned hand He gave me a little enamel image of Himself. Speechless by what had just happened, I could not take my eyes off His gift resting on my palm. Witnessing this for myself was very different from hearing it from others.

"Wait a minute," He added, "let me also give you some *vibhuti*." Saying that He poured the sacred ash from His fingertips, completely covering the enamel image. Overwhelmed, I watched Him wrap it in a bit of paper.

"Don't make it disappear now," I joked, in order not to burst into tears.

"No, no... if I give..."

"I know, I know, I am only joking," I said with a lump in my throat. And we both laughed.

"Call me whenever you need me, I shall hear you no matter what the distance; I shall always be with you. I am yours." These were His parting words.

I bowed down to touch His feet, but He didn't allow me to do so. (It is customary in India to show one's respect to a spiritual leader, a guru, or any venerable person, like parents or elders, in this way.)

Later in the evening Gabriela took me into the temple where *bhajans*[7] were being sung. Everyone sat on the floor, the women on the one side and the men on the other. As if in a dream I heard the melodious chanting, still under the indelible impression of the interview. After a while, Baba entered and sat in an armchair which was on a raised platform. At the end of the last *bhajan*,[8] He rose and everyone stood up to sing the chant of glory, while the priest garlanded him and did the *arati*. After He had left, some people knelt down or prostrated themselves on the floor. Soon the temple doors were closed. They reopened again after a while to allow a stream of women to pour in with their bedding bundled under their arms. In no time at all, the temple was converted into a large dormitory and the lights were turned off.

We then went to the canteen, where I ordered some *dahi* (yoghurt), to the concern of the volunteers who were serving. They thought I should eat something more substantial, but I explained that I always have a light evening meal, generally just yoghurt and fruit. On the way to the guest house I met Mr. Kasturi, of whom the Murphets had spoken a great deal. This friendly elderly man, clad in a white *dhoti*[1] and *kurta*[2] who had been the Principal of Mysore College, was the editor of the monthly magazine of Prasanthi Nilayam, and served as a link between the devotees and Baba.

I did not sleep a wink the whole night, spending it in meditation and a strange state of timelessness. We rose early the next morning and Gabriela took me to the temple at about half-past-four. The *Omkar* started punctually at 5 a.m. *Om* (pronounced A U M), the most sacred and powerful of all the *mantras* (sacred sounds), chanted twenty-one times in the darkness of the temple, made my whole being vibrate in unison with it. I felt as if I was hearing a call from the dim past, a call from another world to which I felt I belonged more that to my earthly surroundings. The very walls seemed to be echoing that sacred sound.

The *Omkar* was followed by the chanting of Sanskrit verses by young boys from the school in clear sweet voices.

"This is the *Suprabhatam*," whispered Gabriela, "to awaken the Gods."

It was not quite clear to me whether she meant the idols slumbering on the altar, or Baba sleeping in His room upstairs above the temple, but I did not ask in order not to hurt her feelings. I was not prepared, at that point, to accept Him as a deity.

A few minutes before 7 a.m., Baba appeared for a moment on the upper balcony to bless the crowd below. After that I left. On the return journey to Bangalore I was seized by a great longing... all I wanted was to be back in the temple to hear the soul-stirring chant of *Om*. "You may never want to leave that place," Mr. Banerji's words came to my mind. And although this was said to me only the previous morning, a great distance lay between the dream of yesterday and the reality of today.

After arriving at the Mysore Palace in Bangalore, I packed my things, leaving half of them in the drawers, something that had never happened to me before during my travels. My hostess, Rani Vijaya, at once noticed a change in me and asked whether I was all right, but I didn't explain. Hesitatingly, I wrote to Baba from Bombay saying that I was glad to have come back from Saigon to meet Him, and was grateful for the interview. But I was unhappy – a feeling that is foreign to my nature. I asked for His help to overcome the depression which prevented me from even meditating. In a state like this I couldn't leave India and go on lecturing, conducting seminars and meditation, counselling and helping people with their various problems and so on.

Putting the unfinished letter into my handbag, I went to do some last minute shopping with Enakshi Bhavnani, my hostess in Bombay and friend of many years. The rush hour had started when we were ready to go home, and there was no chance whatsoever of getting a taxi. We must have stood at the street corner for about fifteen minutes when something least expected suddenly happened. I have no adequate explanations to describe it. The best I can say is it was as if a cloud above had burst and a cascade of brilliant light began to pour down over me like a golden shower. Along with it a sense of untold bliss descended upon me. It was so overpowering that tears of joy began to flow down my cheeks.

"Thank you, Bhagawan," I whispered. "I am so happy!"

"About what, darling?" enquired Enakshi, who must have heard my last words.

But overcome by the ecstatic experience, I was unable to speak or to move. When the downpour of light gradually subsided, leaving me in a cloud of golden mist, a private car suddenly pulled up and its driver took us home. "But it wasn't a taxi," my friend kept thinking. I didn't even feel surprised. I was still not quite back to earth.

The next day I left India radiantly happy. The intensity of that great experience has left a permanent impression. "A momentary state of *samadhi*?" someone suggested. I do not know. I cannot say. I only know that I have not been the same since Sai Baba walked into my life.

End Notes:

1. Author of *Sai Baba – The Man of Miracles*.
2. *Forever Young, Forever Healthy, Yoga for Americans* or *Yoga for You, Renew Your Life Through Yoga* published by Prentice-Hall and translated into ten languages.

    My first book, *Yoga – The Technique of Health* and Happiness, was written and published in India, 1946.
3. The oval-shaped *lingam* is the symbol of the infinite and the principle of creation.
4. *Sai* means Lord, Protector. *Sa* also means divine; *Ai* means mother. *Baba* means father in the universal sense.
5. To behold a holy man which automatically draws his grace on you.
6. This School no longer exists.
7. Means gold in Telugu; here used as a term of endearment.
8. Devotional songs
9. Any one of the Supervisions states possible on the path of Ultimate Realisation; sometimes the Ultimate Realisation itself. Literally 'equal mindedness'; 'the state of god'; 'realised person.'

MY SECOND TRIP
TO PRASANTHI NILAYAM

Ten months later I was back in Prasanthi Nilayam, taking Mr. Murphet's advice not to miss the Maha Shivarathri festival during which Sai Baba publicly performs miracles[1], and has done so for the past twenty-five years. I wanted to see them with my own eyes. That year (1967), Shivarathri fell on 29th March – the darkest night of the year. This festival (literally the 'great Night of Shiva[2]') is celebrated by Hindus all over India. Pious people do not sleep that night, spending it instead in prayer, meditation and in singing *bhajans*. Many of the present westernised Hindus, especially the younger ones, don't care any longer about their religion, or anything for that matter, but some of them do stay awake that night to be on the safe side - 'just in case.' They, however, spend it playing cards, going to the movies or attending parties. It is the way many Westerners nowadays celebrate Christmas and Easter.

On this trip I was accompanied by Bill, my stepson, and his wife. When I introduced her to Sai Baba as my daughter-in-law, He at once remarked, "She is not your daughter-in-law: she is your husband's daughter-in-law." He then turned to the rest of the people He had called into the interview room (we were the only Westerners) and gave a general talk on the oneness of God, no matter by what name people called that Infinite Power.

"There are many bulbs," He said, "but only one current. If the bulb is gone it does not matter, the current is still there. But if there is no current, there is no light – no matter how many bulbs there are. The current is important. The current is one. God is one, people are like bulbs." Taking another example He proceeded: "*Halva, laddus, gulab jamun*[3], all are different sweets, but the basis of them all is sugar. No sugar, no sweets. Similarly, God is the basis of all." He went on explaining that the all pervading Power that is everywhere.

"If you plant a seed into the earth a tree will grow. The tree is not the seed, the leaves are not the seed, but they all grow from the seed. Fruits will grow on the tree, many fruits. Each fruit has again a seed." He took a handkerchief into his hand. "What is this? Cloth. What is cloth? Many threads put together. Pull the threads apart: no cloth, only threads. What is thread? Cotton. Cotton, thread, cloth... What makes cotton into cloth? Work. So is *sadhana* (spiritual practices). Work is worship, duty is God. It is for you to choose whether you want to take the spiritual path... the path to God... or the other path. Take a key... turn it to the right side: the door is open; turn it to the left: the door is closed. Open to spiritual life or closed to spiritual life depends on which way you turn the key."

Addressing Bill He asked: "Who are you?" Getting no answer, He continued: "You don't even know who you are. Is that not important to find out? To find out what is God... where He is?" Finally, He asked the utterly confused young man: "What do you want? You are a Catholic, do you want an image of Christ?" And after circling His hand in the air, He produced a medallion of the Sacred Heart.

When Baba asked my daughter-in-law the same question, she answered, "Nothing." However, He gave her a medallion with His image, since it happened to be what she wanted, but didn't say so. To me He gave some *vibhuti* and promised to see me every day and give me instructions in meditation. I should mention here that not once did He give me that promised instruction, but more a year later He made me conduct the meditation in His temple, and standing beside me, He Himself translated into Telugu what I had been saying in English.

"When did Swami teach you this meditation?" Mr. Kasturi enquired.

"Never!"

"But it is His meditation word by word, lock, stock and barrel."

It occurred to me then that He might have taught it to me in His mysterious way, possibly during my sleep; because when I was conducting the meditation in the temple, it was different from the one I had on my record album.

Since I had come to Puttaparthi a month before Shivaratri, I had the opportunity of witnessing or hearing many first-hand accounts of the miracles performed by Sai Baba. About them, He Himself says: "Don't pay too much importance to *mahimas* (miracles). They are just my *leelas* (divine plays). I first give people what they want, so that later on they may want what I have come to give." And this is very true, because most people who, in the beginning are attracted by His miracles, undergo an inner change with the passage of time, and turn on to the spiritual path.

People who have never even met Baba, have prayed to Him in times of distress, and received succour. One of many examples concerns Kanwarani Balbir Kaur, the step-mother of my next door neighbour, the distinguished and beautiful Maharani of Jind. She, for instance, told me that after two major operations for cancer she started bleeding from the tubes inserted into her abdomen. An immediate third operation was suggested, although it was feared that she may not be able to survive it. In desperation she called for help to Baba, whom she had never seen – only read an article about Him. Two hours later the bleeding had stopped, and new X-rays showed no need for surgery to the bewilderment of the doctors. Soon after, she came to thank Baba for her miraculous recovery. Now she was here again with her step-daughter, Prithwi, the Maharani of Jind, whose daughter, Ratan, was to be married shortly. She had come for Baba's blessings.

In the morning He called all of them for an interview. The Maharani came into my room later, bubbling with excitement, to tell me what had happened. First Baba signed His photo for Ratan, then asked her for her husband's name. Receiving her answer, He chided: "But you are not married. He is not your husband yet. You must always think before speaking." She blushed and bit her tongue. After telling her future and giving His blessings, Baba produced a beautiful necklace of sparkling diamonds and pearls. "You have no father, so I am taking his place and giving you something befitting your status as a princess: this is what he would have given you." Continuing, the Maharani said that everyone was stunned and the girl began to cry. The gift was so sacred to her that she did not want to show it to anyone except me. As I was admiring the exquisite piece of Indian jewellery with five large diamonds and eight smaller ones surrounded by pearls, Prithwi said that she could never afford to give Ratan such a costly present at that time. She also mentioned that "a large pearl fell off the necklace and, although the room was quite bare, we could not find it."

"Never mind", Baba said, "the necklace looks better like this."

"What do you suppose happened to the pearl?", she asked. At that moment I remembered the story Gabriela had told me about the devotee to whom Baba had given a golden medallion with the image of Shirdi Sai Baba. On the way home the man began speculating on the monetary value of the gift, trying to guess how much it would cost. Upon arriving in Bangalore, he opened the box to look at the medallion, but it was not there. Alarmed, he made his way back to Puttaparthi.

"You did not lose it," Baba said after hearing what had happened. "I took it back because you started thinking of its material value instead of its spiritual significance." The culprit fell on his knees and begged to be forgiven. After admonishing him, Baba returned the medallion to him.

Shortly before Shivaratri, Baba came to my room and asked if He could use it for the rehearsal of play which the small boys of the *Veda- Shastra* School were to perform during the festival. I offered to leave, but He didn't want me to. Delighted, I watched the boys sing and act; but when Baba sang a passage to show how it should be done, the performance surpassed everything I had heard about the sweetness of His singing. The rendering of the passage was exceeding dulcet, ethereal and soul-stirring.

I couldn't help remarking: "Sri Krishna charmed people by His flute and You, Bhagawan, by Your voice."

The great day was fast approaching. Thousands of people began pouring into Prasanthi Nilayam; the lucky ones spread their beddings under the trees whereas the rest had to camp under the skies. Shivaratri is celebrated all over India, but it is only in Prasanthi Nilayam that a *Shiva lingam* is 'born' under the very eyes of the thousands of worshippers, when Sai Baba ejects it from His mouth to the ecstatic joy of the assembled multitude. One or more *lingams* are created in Baba's body every Shivaratri, whether He publicly ejects them or not. This glorious emergence is symbolic of Creation taking birth in the Creator.

The morning programme began by Bhagawan hoisting the Prasanthi Nilayam flag on the temple roof, and saying that everyone should hoist in their hearts the flag of Love which destroys evil impulses.

"Practice Yoga, or the mastery of the mind", He urged. "Then the lotus of the heart will bloom, and illumination be attained."

After giving His *Darshan* on the balcony, while *Vedic* hymns were chanted, He spoke on the significance of Maha Shivaratri. He said that this festival is celebrated for the establishment of the Shiva Principle (the Divine Principle) in the heart of man, who alone is endowed with all the necessary qualities to know and enjoy his innate Divinity – his real nature, which is Shiva. But through ignorance and egoism man adopts the path of hate and malice, foregoing his heritage. Only the sages have known the sacredness of human existence, because man alone can become aware of the merging of the *Jivatma*, Individual Consciousness, with *Paramatma*, the Universal Consciousness, and thereby derive lasting happiness.

At ten o'clock the crowd assembled inside and outside the large open shed, which normally serves as a dormitory for the pilgrims, but on festival days is turned into a beautifully decorated auditorium. On the stage a silver statue of Sai Baba of Shirdi was placed on top of a big silver receptacle in the form of a coiled serpent. At eleven o'clock Bhagawan appeared to perform the ceremonial bath of the statue. He first materialised a small figurine of *Ganesh*[4] which he placed on the head Shirdi Baba. He then started the *abishekam*[5] of Shirdi Baba to the continued singing of *bhajans*. By a twirling movement of His hand, He caused an endless stream of *vibhuti* to flow from a small vase upended over the statue. Along with the cascade of sacred ash, some pearls and other precious stones were falling into the silver serpentine urn, filling it to the brim.

Soon after the *abishekam* had started, something strange happened to me. I felt as though I had been transported into another world and was almost unaware of what was going on around me. When I opened my eyes, the place was empty with the exception of a few women who had stayed on to watch over me. They helped me to get to the temple where I wanted to remain alone until I could 'come back to earth' fully.

By six o'clock in the evening all the pilgrims – about 30,000 if not more – had collected in the big open space in front of the *Shanti Vedika* pavillion and were sitting on the ground anxiously waiting to witness the miracle of miracles: the birth of the *Shiva Linga* which emerges from Baba's mouth. This has never been done by anyone, anywhere else in India.

Baba first gave a discourse, mentioning that the *linga* is really the symbol of God since '*lin*' means that in which all beings merge, and '*ga*' means 'the place to which all beings go.' He also explained the inner meaning of *upavasa* which may be interpreted as fasting. But the mere abstention from food is not really what this word conveys. One has also to abstain from bad deeds, words and thoughts because its exact translation is 'living loftily,' that is, 'living in closeness to God.' After ending the talk He led the singing of *bhajans* and stopped singing only shortly before the *lingam* emerged. During the time of the birth of the *linga*, the ecstatic crowd kept on repeating the last line of the *bhajan* sung by Baba before He had to discontinue. When the *linga* finally appeared and fell from His mouth onto the little white towel He was holding up, every heart seemed to beat faster and the crowd burst into a glorious song of praise and rapturous joy. A few minutes later a second *linga* emerged – smaller in size, but of the same amethyst-like colour. After Baba had left, they were placed reverently on a flower-covered tray and the singing of *bhajans* continued throughout the night.

The next morning Baba came out at six O' clock. In His discourse He mentioned that the vigil observed the previous night was a reminder of the vigilance essential to spiritual progress. The fast that is prescribed for *Shivaratri* is not a mere abstention from food, but one should take spiritual food at this time and live in closeness to God, in constant remembrance of His glory and His presence. In conclusion, He stressed the necessity of *dhyana* (meditation). After the *arati* was done to Him, food was distributed to break the fast.

I volunteered to help serve the people – with rice cooked with vegetables, followed by sweet rice, on plates made of dried leaves.

"How could the ashram kitchen prepare food for 30,000 when its capacity is limited to eight or nine hundred meals?" I asked one of the volunteers.

"We cook to our capacity," was the answer, "and when the food is ready, Swami touches the vessels so that they should not get empty until everyone has been served."

"And you do not run out of food?"

"Not when He touches it. Why are you so surprised?" The young man asked. "Didn't Christ feed a multitude with five loaves of bread and two fish?"

I wanted to know what would happen to the *lingam* which Baba had produced. I was told that He usually gave them away to one or another of His devotees. The following day, my new friend, Prithwi, the Maharani of Jind, came into the room looking far from her usual composed self. At first I couldn't make out what she was saying.

"The *linga*... the *Shiva linga*... Swami gave it to me" and opening her bag she showed the *lingam* wrapped in a handkerchief. It looked like a beautiful translucent amethyst, the size and shape of a large 'egg.' Excited and overwhelmed by this act of Baba's grace, she packed her suitcases and hurriedly left.

There is an interesting sequel to this incident. About two years later, we were sitting at Baba's feet in the small room below the one where He usually takes His meals. It was a few days after He had cured Tara, a young girl of about eighteen, who after getting an antibiotic for some intestinal trouble suddenly became paralysed. She had been bedridden for five years, her body completely stiff and unable to move. Finally she was brought to Baba who gave her some *vibhuti* to be taken with a little water. Since her condition remained unchanged, her elder brothers brought her again to Prasanthi Nilayam. This time Bhagawan gave her a *rudraksa* (a seed) saying that a spoonful of water should be poured over it each day and that she should then drink that water. This did not help either. When she was taken to Prasanthi Nilayam for the third time, Bhagawan motioned the brothers to bring her to the interview room. In less than two minutes Tara came out to the loud cheers of the crowd hailing Sai Baba and slowly walked three times around the temple, aided only by her mother and sister.

Bringing up this incident, Prithwi asked Swami why He cured Tara during her third visit, when He could have done it the first time.

"It was necessary in her case," He explained, "because she still had to pay off a bit of her *karmic* debt.[6] Also, I did it to strengthen the faith of her family and to test it. Her brothers didn't waver and continued to believe in My promise to cure her."

At the end of our interview, Bhagawan told Prithwi that since she had started a business, it would be better if she gave back the *Shiva linga* in exchange for another one, because she didn't have the time to attend to it properly and perform the necessary rituals and *abishekam* which this *linga* requires. If this is not done the *linga* brings bad luck to the owner. Prithwi admitted having had an extremely unfortunate year, yet she felt reluctant to part with the *linga*. While I was trying to persuade her to do so, she took the treasure out of her handbag and kept looking at it, hesitating to return it to Baba.

Meanwhile, Baba got up and went to the winding staircase ready to go upstairs, when Prithwi, having finally decided, wrapped the *lingam* in a handkerchief and stretched out her hand for Baba to take it. Instead of taking it, He held His hand under hers for a moment and then said that it was now all right to open the handkerchief. "Ah!" was all she could mutter at the sight of a small golden *lingam*, complete with a *pita* (a square stand on which it is usually placed) Both of us just stood still, hardly believing our eyes. The silence was broken by a rhythmical hammering sound coming from upstairs. I looked up wondering what it could be, when suddenly I saw the unbelievable... the *Shiva lingam* was 'walking' down, step by step, making a thudding sound each time it hit the steep stone stairs! Speechless, we watched it slowly come down and stop at the feet of Bhagawan. "My *lingam*," exclaimed Prithwi as He turned around and went upstairs. We both looked for the *lingam*, but it had vanished. "Can you beat that?" said my friend, shaking her head.

A few days after the festival, Baba was due in Bombay and, to my great joy, I was to go with him. He also took along the forty-four schoolboys who were to perform in Bombay the play, from the life of Sri Krishna, which they had enacted in Puttaparthi during Shivaratri. It was the first time they were leaving the village, and they were very excited when the bus turned off the dirt road on to a paved one – what a novelty it was for them!

Whenever we halted on the way, Baba's car would immediately be surrounded by people trying to catch a glimpse of Him, to get His blessings and, if possible, to touch His feet. We stopped for lunch in Hampi at a three hundred year old

Vishnu temple now turned into a guest house by the Government. It was here, in Hampi, that the young Sai was seen standing on the altar of the Veerupaksha temple in front of the *lingam*, although he had not even been inside the temple.

Upon arriving in Bombay, we all stayed with Baba in a large, old house, the Modi bungalow, just outside the city. Every morning *bhajans* were sung by devotees gathered under the *pandal* (tent) erected in front of the house. The crowd gradually swelled from approximately six thousand to ten or twelve thousand – the overflow sitting on the streets outside the gate. At nine o'clock Baba would usually come out and walk among the people, along the roped-off passages, across the length and breadth of the entire jam-packed area. He would always walk up to the last row, even outside the gate, so that everyone could get His *Darshan*. He would bless books, photos, flowers or other objects held up by hundreds of people; or take letters from them in which all sorts of favours were asked of Him – from cures to jobs, from *moksha* (liberation) to babies.

"How can He read all those letters?" I wondered aloud.

"He doesn't have to," answered Mr. Kasturi, "He knows what is in them at the time when they were written and He answers them in His inimitable way. Not necessarily in words, but by granting the wishes if the time is right."

When watching though the window as He moved silently among the crowd, tears would come to my eyes, although I seldom cry. Even now, whenever I see Him moving amongst the people, silent and aloof, yet aware of their most intimate desires and wishes, I am still moved to tears.

Dr. Ramakrishna Rao, who arrived a few days after us, was staying in the guest room next to ours. A noted scholar and former Governor of Kerala and Uttar Pradesh, His Excellency was a friendly, elderly man and a humble devotee of Bhagawan.

He came to translate Baba's discourses from Telugu into Hindi at the public meetings which were held at the Sports Stadium. Incidentally, whenever the interpreter happened to stop for a moment in search of a word, Baba would whisper it to him to the great delight of the audience. Having heard of two unusual incidents in his life, I asked Dr. Rao to verify them.

The first happened at the time when he was Governor of Uttar Pradesh and was travelling in a special train carriage with his wife. His A.D.C. and retinue had already retired for the night in the next carriage, when all of a sudden he noticed sparks coming from the fan on the ceiling. These grew rapidly in volume, and threatened to set the compartment on fire. There was no alarm cord to stop the train and no connecting passage with the other carriages. The doors opened directly on to the station platform or, at that moment, on to the darkness of the night. The train was moving at full speed and there seemed no hope for them. Feeling trapped and expecting the worst, they both began to pray to Baba, when they heard a knock at the door. The Governor was surprised, but opened it to see a mechanic, who, without saying a word, went to work on the fire spitting fan. After repairing it, he sat on the floor and suggested they continue their night's rest, but the lady objected suspecting the man to be a thief. Who else would be walking on the running board of a moving train at night? The mechanic then got up and opening the door vanished into the night, leaving the couple utterly amazed.

The other incident happened several weeks later. Dr. Rao was flying on official business in a government plane to Banares accompanied by his wife, A.D.C. and some other officials. When they were above Banares the pilot informed them that something had gone wrong and the wheels would not come down, making landing impossible. The pilot kept circling the airport trying to make the lever work, until he almost ran out of fuel. Again, all of them started praying to Bhagawan for help. The A.D.C., who was also a devotee, was wearing a ring given to him by Baba and asked if he could try his luck with the lever. No sooner had he put his hand on it, than the wheels came down without any difficulty. The next day the Governor's wife phoned Baba to thank Him for rescuing them.

"You are mentioning only the plane and saying nothing about the train," said Baba, giving full details of both incidents.

I was grateful to His Excellency for giving me a personal account of these stories which once more proved Baba's care and concern for his devotees, as well as His omnipresence and omnipotence.

That week with Bhagawan in Bombay passed like a fairy tale, each day bringing something unexpected and wondrous. One morning He came to the verandah outside our rooms followed by Mr. Java, a prominent member of the Bombay Samithi (committee), who was trying to slip on to his finger a ring which Baba had given him, but it was a little tight. The rest of us were looking on at his struggle as we sat on the floor along the wall opposite Baba's chair. Baba asked Java for the ring, promising to make it larger. He gave it to the person nearest him and when it reached me I handed it to Bhagawan. Taking the ring, He just blew on it and returned it to me saying that now it would fit but it was changed a little. Glancing at it, I almost lost my breath: nine precious stones had suddenly appeared around the enamel image on the ring.

"That is nothing," my companion remarked, "I have seen Him return sight to a blind man by just blowing into his eyes." This, however, didn't surprise me as much as the ring, probably because there is a great difference between seeing something yourself and hearing someone else's account.

In the afternoon Mr. Java brought a cake which Baba was to cut for all of us who had gathered in the large living room. I was one of the first to receive a big slice, but figuring that the medium-sized cake would never suffice for everyone, I put my plate on the windowsill meaning to give it to those left out. "Not when He cuts it," said Mrs. Java, to whom my intention was explained. She was right. Not only all of us, including the forty-four schoolboys, but every volunteer in the garden and the kitchen staff – over a hundred people in all – received very generous portions, and still there was quite a bit left over.

The morning before my departure, as I was packing my suitcase, Bhagawan came into our room. Expressing regret for not having had time to give me the promised interview, he asked whether I wanted some *vibhuti*. Who would refuse such an offer? He then blew into his closed fist three times and then opened it holding out to me a small round silver box.

"*Vibhuti, akshaya patra.*" (a box with an inexhaustible supply of *vibhuti*) I was surprised and happy at this unexpected gift. I had heard that Baba once gave *vibhuti* to a devotee who was leaving for England and promised that the quantity would last for the duration of her stay abroad, but I never expected that this would happen to me.

As soon as Baba left, almost the entire household, including the cooks from downstairs, came to my room asking me to give them a pinch of the *vibhuti* which they either swallowed at once, or mixed with ordinary *vibhuti* brought in a package, so that it should acquire the miraculous properties of His gift.

However that wasn't all The next morning Baba lit a temple lamp for my intended Crusade for Light, and produced a silver medallion with His image engraved on it. Since I don't wear jewellery, He suggested I keep it in my handbag.

"Be happy," He blessed me at parting.

End Notes:
1. *Bhagawan would produce (a) lingam(s) from His mouth, and bathe a Shirdi Sai statue with vibhuti from an empty pot as His 'usual' miracles on Shivaratri. He had discontinued both practices since the late seventies, when, suddenly on Shivaratri morning in February 99, He produced the Hiranyagarbha Lingam in public view.*
2. *The Hindu Trinity consists of Brahma, the Creator; Vishnu, the Preserver, and Shiva, the Destroyer.*
3. *Indian sweets.*
4. *The elephant headed god, the son of Shiva and Parvati, who is a mythological figure, symbolising wisdom and strength. Shiva never incarnated, but the sages of olden times knew that it is difficult for people to worship a formless God, so they endowed Shiva figure with a wife and two sons. The same goes for Vishnu and Brahma. It is much like the Christians worshipping God, the Father, incarnate in God, the son, Jesus.*
5. *Ablution.*
6. *To pay for sins committed in a previous birth.*

MIRACULOUS EXPERIENCES

While I was at Puttaparthi, I was able to meet, through Mr. Kasturi's kindness, people whose experiences with Baba were especially noteworthy. One was Dr. S. Dakshinamurti, Head of the Agricultural Physics Division at the Indian Agricultural Research Institute in New Delhi. He recounted how he had met Bhagawan and come to believe in Him:

"It was in 1962, before I ever knew anything about Sai Baba, that I began seeing a strange vision. Whenever I was in any kind of predicament or needed to solve a scientific problem, the 'visitor' was there. Finally I related this strange occurrence to my senior colleague, Dr. S. Bhagawantham, Scientific Adviser to the Government of India, who immediately recognised whose image I was seeing. He suggested that I must meet Sai Baba and invited me to Hyderabad where he himself was due to meet Him. That is how I first met Him and recognised Him instantly.

"When I was left alone with Baba He told me that twenty-five years ago I had wanted to come to Puttaparthi, but did so only in a dream. I was taken aback and remembered that when I was in Kurnool I heard about a youth who cured people and performed other miracles in Puttaparthi. The village was close by, and though I didn't go there, I did dream I visited it.

"I am now His humble devotee. Wherever I go I carry Swami in my heart and always turn to Him for advice and guidance, whether in research, official matters or domestic problems."

While Dr. Dakshinamurti was in Hyderabad for a dedication ceremony at Dr. Bhagawantham's house, the host himself was delayed. Baba, to everyone's surprise, suggested that they should not wait for him but to go ahead with the ceremony, because Dr. Bhagawantham was in the Himalayas and would not arrive in time. They later learned that the plane had some trouble and was, in fact, flying over the Himalayas at the time Baba made that announcement.

I was also told of the incident when Dr. Dakshinamurti was attending a Conference of the International Atomic Agency in Ankara. He was unexpectedly asked to preside. Not being prepared for this, he prayed to Bhagawan for help. As he took the chair he saw before him Baba's raised palm with some important points for his speech written on it.

Another visitor brought to my room by my 'big brother,' Mr. Kasturi, was a man in whose house Baba's photo was producing *vibhuti*. Formerly a thief, Halagappa had reformed when Swami spotted him in a crowd and told him to give up his 'profession' and take a job which would be provided for him. He was now working as a mechanic in a sugar factory. When Halagappa came to my room bringing with him a large coffee can full of *vibhuti*, he gave a heaped spoonful to every one of the ten people sitting in my room. Closing the can, he turned it upside down several times, murmuring something. When he lifted the lid again, we looked at each other in amazement, for the can was full to the top! The next day I wrote down an account of what had happened and asked all those who had seen it with me, to sign in verification. I felt sure that otherwise no one at home would believe this had actually happened. In the evening Halagappa returned with yet another can – this time with sweet *vibhuti* in it. He told us that he used to gather the ashes from Baba's picture in his house and mix it with sugar before offering it to people when they flocked to his humble dwelling. One day his wife remarked that they couldn't afford the sugar so they decided to do without it. The next morning when, as usual, they took a pinch of *vibhuti* from the photo, they were surprised to find that it was sweet. Again he gave a liberal portion to each one of us and again the container mysteriously replenished itself.

We were very grateful to him for sharing his experience and gift with us, and wishing to thank him, we pulled out some money and heaped it in front of him.

"No, no, no," he shook his head when we offered it to him, tears rolling down his cheeks. Feeling very uncomfortable about our well-meant offer, we quickly took back the money. The same day Halagappa bought a cheap, plastic ring in the bazaar with Baba's image on it. After wearing it for a while he felt that his hand had become wet and sticky. He was thunderstruck upon finding that it was *amrita*, the nectar which Bhagawan gives to His devotees on some festival days. He was shaken by this act of Baba's grace, bestowed on him probably because he had withstood the temptation of money by not accepting ours. He placed the ring in an empty jar and the nectar began to increase in volume. A few days later he gave us all small bottles full of nectar to take home.

Mr. Ramakant Potdar, of Ulhasnagar, related to me the story of a poor woman who came to their home frequently to borrow money. Her husband had been constrained to sell everything they possessed to pay off his debts. One day she unexpectedly came to repay some of the money she owed and also asked for Baba's photo. She explained that the last time she had come to borrow money, she had been extremely upset by the thought that she would be unable to repay it. In despair she prayed to Baba for help. Two days later her husband returned home at night with two cows he had found by the roadside. The next day he and other neighbours attempted to trace the owner. All the villagers were alerted, but no one ever showed up to claim the cows. By selling their milk the couple had now been able to reinstate themselves, for which they were grateful to Bhagawan.

MY THIRD TRIP
TO SEE BABA

In less than five months after returning from India, I was on my way back there again, because the medallion which Baba had given to me in Bombay had mysteriously disappeared. My husband, Dr. Sigfrid Knauer, M.D., who besides being an outstanding physician is a most wonderful and unique person, suggested that possibly Baba wanted me to go to India.

"You wouldn't have come otherwise," Swami said with a mischievous twinkle in his eyes, when I told Him about the disappearance of His gift upon arriving in Prasanthi Nilayam.

"Oh, Bhagawan!" was all that I could say to this unusual way of calling me to His side.

During this, my third visit to Puttaparthi, I volunteered to teach *yoga asanas* to the boys of His School, the Veda-Shastra Patashala. He took a keen interest in the classes and would usually be present at the lessons to the great delight of all the participants including myself.

That year, 1967, Krishna Jayanti (Krishna's birthday) was celebrated on 27th and 28th August and Bhagawan asked me to speak in the Temple on this occasion. After garlanding Him and doing *Padanamaskar* (touching His feet in reverence), I spoke on the birth of Sri Krishna and said that, although this event took place over five thousand years ago, He still lives in the hearts of His devotees who know Him through scriptures, legends, songs, poems and paintings. Continuing, I said that an event which had taken place many centuries ago, was again taking place in our midst. All the miracles which had been performed then are again being performed now. However, a sophisticated, westernised Hindu is not likely to take them seriously and would probably scoff at them. At the conclusion of my speech, I read a passage from the *Srimad Bhagavatam* about Sri Krishna, which closely fitted the description of Baba:

"He who is all-pervading, infinite and omnipresent, the controller of all, permits Himself to be controlled by those who love Him. Not by penance, nor by austerities nor by studies, is He attained; but those who love Him with whole-souled devotion, find Him easily, for they are His chosen, they who have pure love in their hearts. Infinite though He is, he may be realised through love."

The visit to Prasanthi Nilayam gave me the chance to witness and realise the tremendous impact of the kind of love Bhagawan exudes and showers on everyone. He overwhelms you with it and it radiates from Him like warmth radiates from the sun, spontaneous and never ceasing. At the same time, when it comes to spiritual practices and disciplines, He can be a hard taskmaster. As He says:

"You are My treasure, even if you deny Me. I am your treasure, even if you say 'No.' I shall take endless trouble to keep my property safe in My custody – that is to say in the custody of the Lord, by whichever name you may call Him – all the powers I have are for you. I am just the storekeeper, keeping them ready to be given to you, whenever you ask for them. My *prema* (love) shall be given even if you do not ask, for it is your right to share in it. Some complain that I did not give them this or that, but they do so because their vision is limited to the immediate future or the present, whereas I know what is in store for them and so I have to safe-guard them from greater grief. They even blame Me and heap abuses on me, but I will not give them up. I am not influenced by anybody, remember. There is no one who can change My course or affect My conduct to the slightest extent.

I am the Master over all. I speak harshly and punish some persons only because I have *prema* towards them and I am eager to correct them and make them better instruments.

"Continue your worship of your chosen God along the lines already familiar to you. Then you will find that you are coming nearer and nearer to Me, for all names are Mine and all forms are Mine. There is no need to change your chosen God and adopt a new one when you have seen Me and heard Me.

"For the protection of the virtuous, for the destruction of evil-doers and for establishing righteousness on a firm footing, I incarnate from age to age. At the present time, strife and discord have robbed peace and unity from the family, the school, the community, the society, villages, the cities and the State. The arrival of the Lord was also anxiously awaited by saints and sages. *Sadhus* prayed and I have come. My main tasks are fostering of the *Vedas* and fostering of the devotees. Your virtue, your self-control, your detachment, your faith, your steadfastness, these are the signs by which people read of My glory. You can lay claim to be My devotee only when you have placed yourself in My hands fully and completely, with no trace of ego. You can enjoy the bliss through the experience the *Avatar* confers. The *Avatar* behaves in a human way so that mankind can feel kinship, but rises into his super-human heights so that mankind can aspire to reach the heights, and through that aspiration can actually reach Him.

"Every step in the career of the *Avatar* is pre-determined. Rama came to feed the roots of *sathya* (truth) and *dharma* (righteousness). Krishna came to foster *shanti* (peace) and *prema* (love). Now all these four are in danger of drying up. And that is why the present Avatar has come. I have come to correct the *buddhi* (intelligence) – by various means. I have to counsel, help, command, condemn and stand by as a friend and well-wisher to all, so that they may give up evil propensities and, recognising the straight path, tread it and reach the goal. I have to reveal to the people the worth of the *Vedas*, the *Shastras* and other spiritual texts, which lay down the customs.

"I have come to give you the key to the treasure of *ananda* (bliss), and to tell you how to tap that spring, for you have forgotten the way of blessedness. If you waste this chance of saving yourselves, it is just your fate. You come to get from Me tinsel and trash, the petty little solutions and promotions, worldly joys and comforts. Very few of you desire to get from Me the thing I have come to give you – liberation itself. Come, examine, experience and have faith."

Towards the end of my stay in Prasanthi Nilayam, Bhagawan called me for an interview together with a few other ladies. Pleased with the progress the boys had made in *yoga asanas*, He produced a ring with a sapphire in the middle and seven golden rays with little diamonds at the ends.

"Seven rays of virtue," He explained.

When in my room, I mused over the ring, not being sure as to what I should do with it. I had given up wearing jewels since 1939, when I left India and started teaching Yoga in Shanghai. If the ring had His image, I thought to myself, I would not have minded wearing it.

The next day, all of us were called again into the interview room. As soon as we were settled on the floor, He stretched out His hand.

"Give me back the ring, *acha nahi hai*" (it is not a nice one). Holding it by the gold band, he simply blew on it, and lo!... a single, sparkling diamond shone on the ring. The blue stone and rays had disappeared.

Putting it on my finger, Bhagawan said, "You wanted to have one with my image, didn't you?".

"Yes," I nodded.

"Everytime you wish, you will see Me in the ring, but no one else will. Wear it for safety, especially when you go out. It will let Me know should you be in danger and be in need of My protection."

"You have given me so much, Bhagawan," I uttered hesitatingly, touching His feet, "I don't know how to thank You for everything, but I came here to get back my medallion."

"This one?" He smiled, holding it up in His hand before returning it to me.

The following morning He took me along to Hyderabad where Dr. Ramakrishna Rao was on his death-bed and kept calling all the time to his Lord in his delirium.

"I can, of course, come to him at anytime, but for the sake of the family I think that I should go in My physical form," said Baba.

We stopped for a picnic lunch under the shade of a few trees a little distance from the highway. Although no buildings or people could be seen, we were soon surrounded by a group of villagers, rapidly growing in number, who appeared seemingly from nowhere. Bhagawan gave some *vibhuti* to woman with a sickly-looking baby, whereupon everybody immediately crowded around Him with outstretched palms. This kind of scene invariably repeats itself, when His car happens to halt on a road, no matter how deserted it may be. Passing buses then usually stop to allow the passengers to have His *Darshan*, the lucky ones managing to touch His feet, the hem of his robe or the dust on which He trod.

During the eight hour drive, we sang *bhajans*, meditated in silence, or asked some questions of Bhagawan. I, for example, wanted Him to verify a story I had heard once about a necklace which he had given to a famous singer after she had performed for Him and the assembled pilgrims during one of the festivals. I was told that the singer's husband had secretly taken Baba's gift to a jeweller for valuation, but when he opened the box he found it was empty. The necklace then appeared on the statue of Sri Krishna in the temple at Prasanthi Nilayam.

"This is true," Bhagawan said, "only the necklace didn't appear on Krishna's statue, but came back to Me. We were all sitting in My room; Raja Reddy and others, when this happened."

Taking this opportunity, I also asked what happens to a gift which He has given to a devotee when the devotee dies.

"It goes to the family."

"And if there is no family, can it possibly get into the wrong hands?".

"Never. In that case it will come back to me. Don't worry," He added with a gentle smile, guessing that I had in mind the ring He had given me.

In Hyderabad, all of us stayed in the house of Mr. Sathyamurti and his father Krishnamurti. Bhagawan went immediately to see Dr. Ramakrishna Rao, who regained consciousness as soon as He entered the room. The dying devotee murmured that now, after receiving His Lord's blessings, he was ready to leave in peace.

The same thing happened to Mr. Kasturi's old mother. Before passing away, she opened her eyes and told the family: "Now I can go, Swami just came and gave me the *thirtam* (water)." No one else had seen Him, but to her His presence was a reality.

Several others have told me that Baba always appears to His devotees at the time when they breathe their last, making their transition happy and fearless.

"Will you also come to me at my 'going time'?" I once asked Bhagawan.

"Do you have any doubts?" He asked.

On the way back to Puttaparthi, Baba suddenly decided to go to Bangalore from where my plane was leaving. Needless to say, I was more than delighted to spend the night at Brindavan, His summer residence outside Bangalore.

The next evening, I returned to the palace where my hostess, Rani Vijaya, had guests for dinner. During the course of the conversation, I made a mention of Rama, Krishna, Buddha and Indian deities.

"I am afraid I do not know these gentlemen," remarked a young man among the guests.

"You had better find out something about them," I retorted. Apparently, he was anxious to pose as an ultra-modern, sophisticated individual as many other people do in India nowadays. They want to disassociate themselves from their religion, traditions and customs, trying blindly to copy westerners, especially Americans, often making themselves both pitiful and ridiculous. Oddly enough this is happening at a time when many westerners, tired of the rat race and materialistic pursuits, are turning their eyes towards India in the hope of finding an answer to their search for a more meaningful, spiritual way of life. At present there are probably more Americans who spend their time in meditation and in studying the ancient culture of India than Indians themselves. That is one of the reasons why Sai Baba is anxious to establish His colleges all over India, so that boys and girls can, in addition to the usual curriculum, learn something about the spiritual and cultural heritage of their country.

BABA CALLS ME AGAIN

Soon after returning home, I began lecturing on Bhagawan and showing a film of the Shivaratri festival. Once during the question and answer period a man from the audience said: "And do you expect us to believe you!"

"No, I don't," I admitted. "At first I didn't believe it either, I am only sharing with you my incredible experiences and hope that you will disbelieve me so whole-heartedly, that you yourself will make a trip to Baba and obtain your own experiences."

"If Sai Baba can multiply food," I am invariably asked by my audiences, "why doesn't he feed the hungry masses of India?"

"Did Christ do it? Did any of the Divine Beings or great saints do it?" I usually counter-question. "His mission is a spiritual one, and feeding the population is the business of the government. Sai Baba has come to bring the message of love, to uphold righteousness, to uphold truth, to turn people onto a spiritual path and make them realise their Divine origin."

"How do you know that Sai Baba is an *Avatar*?" Is another question I am frequently asked.

"The same way you would know the difference between a great artist and a mediocrity: by your experience."

"Are you God?" A man once asked Baba during an interview.

"Yes," He replied, "and so are you. Only I know it and you don't."

When I came back to Tecate everyone, including my husband and students, were quite surprised at seeing me wearing a diamond ring. But to me it was not a piece of jewellery but Bhagawan's gift, and should He choose to turn it into a grey pebble I would have worn it like my mother's seven carat diamond, the only one she was able to save when leaving Russia during the Revolution. Somehow, it wasn't me who gave up wearing jewels and gaudy saris after completing my Yoga training with Shri Krishnamacharya in Mysore, but rather the other way around – they gave me up!

Talking about Baba's ring, I can actually see Him in it, sometimes even what He is doing, not as in a movie, but rather as on a slide. Checking later with Mr. Kasturi I found that what I was seeing did match with the facts. "Are you spying on him?" jokingly asked my 'big brother' after we had finished comparing notes.

It wasn't too long that I remained at home. On 19th February 1968 I was again getting ready to go to India, this time with about twelve people who, after attending my lectures, were eager to meet Sai Baba.

Upon landing in Delhi, we intended to spend the following day sight-seeing. But apparently Bhagawan wanted us to come to Puttaparthi, because early the next morning I called Dr. Bhagawantham. I had not even met him though I had heard about him from various people. He suggested that we go immediately to Prasanthi Nilayam in order not to miss the celebrations of the Vaikunta Ekadasi. He was still the Scientific Adviser to the Defence Ministry in the Government of India. We finally met on the plane from Delhi.

I was very interested to hear what he had to say about the way he became Baba's devotee. To begin with, the scientist had no desire whatsoever to see someone who, as he thought then, impresses the gullible public by means of some magic tricks. It so happened that he met Sai Baba at the home of one of his relatives. Bhagawan invited him to Prasanthi Nilayam and he went, cynical of Him. During his stay they both went for a stroll along the river outside Puttaparthi and Baba, knowing what was going on in the scientist's mind, told him to choose a place where they could sit down by the riverside. He then asked whether he, as a scientist, still had any regard for the *Bhagavad Gita*. Receiving an affirmative answer, Baba asked whether he would like a copy of it.

Dr. Bhagawantham assured him that he would treasure it. Then, Baba unexpectedly plunged His hands into the stream apparently to scoop some water, but when He stretched them out He had in them a beautifully bound volume of the *Gita*. Dr. Bhagawantham was stunned and, after thanking Him for this unexpected gift, instinctively turned the first page to see where the book had been printed. Noticing this, Baba smiled and said, pointing to the region of His solar plexus, "At the Sai Press."

It took Dr. Bhagawantham two years of watching, examining and weighing Sai's words and deeds before he could finally accept Him as a Divinity, an *Avatar*, who is beyond any human understanding or scientific explanation. Now, when he is not busy with his official work or away attending conferences, he acts as Baba's interpreter at lectures and discourses, translating them meticulously from Telugu into English.

Our group arrived in Prasanthi Nilayam just in time for the Vaikunta Ekadasi celebrations. Everyone was thrilled to hear Baba leading the singing of the *bhajans*, so far they had heard His voice only on tapes and records. But much more was in store for them. After the *bhajans* the crowd from the temple joined those sitting outside and formed orderly rows to wait for Baba. He came out, followed by a Brahmin carrying a silver chalice filled with *amrita*. Scooping it out with a big round spoon, Baba went along the lines of several thousand people, pouring the fragrant nectar into the cupped palms of all those present without ever refilling the container. Thus my wish to see this wonder came true several years after Gabriela told me about it during my first visit to the Ashram.

The following evening another dream was fulfilled. Standing by Bhagawan's side, I conducted the meditation on Light. We continued this for a week, after which the meditation was to be done in silence and ended by chanting in chorus the Sanskrit verse:

> *Asatoma sat gamaya,*
> *Tamasoma jyotir gamaya,*
> *Mrityorma amritam gamaya.*
> *Shanti, shanti, shanti.*

(From the unreal to the Real, from darkness to Light, from death to Immortality. Peace, peace, peace.)

It was so beautiful that I wanted to record it. Since I was sitting in the first row, I threw my sari over the tape recorder, and quietly switched it on just before the chant was to be started. Suddenly, a loud shrieking sound pierced the silence. I quickly stopped the machine, held my breath and wished I could just sink through the floor. Mercifully Bhagawan never said a word about it.

Before calling the group of thirteen Americans for an interview, He sent beautiful saris for the ladies, which made them look more presentable since one cannot sit cross-legged in mini-dresses. There was an awkward silence in the room when Baba came in, but He quickly put everyone at ease by asking: "Will you eat some Indian sweets if I give them to you?" Receiving a timid "yes" for an answer, He made a few circling movements in the air with His right hand and began distributing the most delicious sweets. "Freshly prepared," He smiled, "eat them." The ice was broken and everybody started laughing while licking their fingers.

Welcoming the group, Baba said that He was still busy with devotees from the festival crowd, but that He would be seeing us daily later on, since we had come from so far. Spotting Elsie Cowan, who was suffering from severe headaches, and Walter, who had diabetes, He gave each of them something to relieve their pain. "And to Indra Devi I shall give a *japa-mala* (bead necklace) which she will be able to use for curing people who come to her for help." Saying this, he moved His hand as usual getting hold of a long string of beads from nowhere.

"What are they?" someone asked, looking at the unusual rosary still swinging in His hand.

"Pearls," Bhagawan answered.

"First time I ever saw pearls taken from the air instead of from the sea," a businessman remarked.

"One hundred and eight of them, and all the same size," Baba added, guessing what was on the man's mind, who later admitted to us that he was wondering how much time a jeweller would have to spend to match so many pearls. Placing the *mala* around my neck, Baba said: "I am endowing it with healing powers." In deep gratitude I touched His feet with my forehead and asked if the *japa-mala* would heal any condition.

"No, not if the illness is a form of payment for a *karmic* debt.... for misdeeds committed in a previous life," he answered. "In such a case, even I will not touch that person. One should not interfere with the law of *karma*. The *mala* also will not cure such cases."

The *japa-mala* created quite a stir in Prasanthi Nilayam. Wherever I walked, people would ask me to show it to them and then would reverently press it against their eyes. The healings subsequently performed by the *japa-mala* were so numerous, that I do not even recall them, except a few. One of the most outstanding cases was that of my Mexican student, Rosa de L., who came to me before a biopsy was to be performed to determine whether a uterine tumour was benign or malignant. She feared the worst and asked to be healed by the *japa-mala*. Several days later she rang me up, crying with joy, to tell me that the tumour had completely disappeared, baffling the doctor.

Keeping His promise to the group, Baba used to come to the guest house, where all of us were assembled in my room, at about ten o'clock, everyday. He spent about an hour with us and gave us instructions, answered our questions, spoken and unspoken, bringing out some minute details of the hidden thoughts and wishes in our minds. And all this with so much love, patience and compassion, that it is difficult to describe. He often used parables and little stories to convey better the depth of the Indian religious philosophy and of His own teachings to a western mind, since no one else in the group had been in India before, besides me, of course.

Speaking about different religions, He said: "Love of the Lord should not degenerate into fanaticism, into a hatred of other names and forms. This type of cancer is affecting even eminent men. Avoid this by believing that all those who revere the Lord are your brothers, even if their outer appearance, language, skin colour, and the methods they adopt to express their reverence are different from yours. God is only one."

Again: "Take, for example, gold, out of which a jeweller makes various ornaments – earrings, bracelets, chains, rings and broaches – they are all different articles, but all are made of the same gold."

Or: "When admiring a garland you see only the various flowers, you don't see the thread which keeps them together. But without it, they will all fall apart and there will be no garland. God is that thread and you the flowers."

"Religion is a personal encounter of the individual with the Supreme. Do not unsettle anyone's faith. God is one. Each comes from God and is of God himself. Each individual is a flower in the garden of God. Annihilation of the ego and the dissolution of desires must be done here and now, otherwise a return to this transient world is sure."

"You can look at the reflection in the mirror, take away the mirror, there will be no reflection. You don't need a reflection – you are God. If a bird is sitting on a very thin branch, which the wind is blowing up and down, the bird is not afraid because it has faith in the Higher Self."

After staying about a week in Puttaparthi, I went to Kerala with Baba's blessing to lecture there at the request of Justice B. Eradi (the state president of the Sai Samithi of Kerala) and other devotees there. While driving through Chikbalapur with two of my students and the Rajkumar (Prince) of Sandur at the wheel, we met with a frightening accident. A little girl, running across the street, bumped her head against our car and fell down bleeding profusely from the mouth. Muriel Engle, sitting at the back, kept repeating "Baba, save her! Baba, save her!" while the crowd around us grew restless and hostile. We drove the girl along with her father to the hospital. The doctor found that she was not hurt badly and the blood came from her slightly bruised lips and teeth. Grateful for a happy ending to what could have been a serious case, we drove away singing *bhajans* in praise.

In my beloved Kerala, I was overwhelmed by the enthusiastic reception given in Palghat, Trichur and Ernakulam, where the lecture halls overflowed with Baba's devotees and the general public. It was such an open demonstration of love and loyalty to Baba that even those who came out of curiosity to hear what a foreigner had to say about Sai Baba and Yoga, whole-heartedly participated in the offering of homage to Him.

On the way back to Prasanthi Nilayam, I stopped for a few days in Bangalore to visit the great Russian painter Svetoslav Roerich and his beautiful Indian wife Devika Rani. Another guest, besides me, was a young man who, upon learning about my *japa-mala*, told me that he had seen it, or at least one like it, some ten years ago when Sai Baba and His party came to Kanya Kumari (Cape Comorin). As they all stood on the shore, a wave brought out to Baba's feet a pearl necklace from the ocean. "It looked exactly like yours," he finished his story, pensively shaking his head.

I returned to Prasanthi Nilayam just before Dr. M. C. Modi, the famous opthalmologist, was to conduct a Free Eye Treatment Camp which was sponsored by Baba. Because of His presence and by His grace, the doctor was able to perform five hundred and eleven operations, mostly for cataract, instead of the proposed two hundred. Over three thousand semi-blind villagers came to the Camp. Three hundred volunteers from among the devotees at the Ashram and the older boys of the school, none of whom had ever had any nursing experience before, were to help look after the patients. By merely speaking to them, Baba was able, within an hour, to 'train' them.

It was quite an experience to observe the entire procedure. From Dr. Modi's fast examinations to the blitz-like operations, after which the people patiently lay still until the bandages were removed a few days later. The volunteers carried the patients into the sheds and cared for them during the post-operative period. Baba was all over the place, supervising, instructing and helping. By using mats and *dhotis* – sheets were not available in Puttaparthi – He Himself made beds on the floor for those who didn't bring their own bedding. Most people in the South, where it is warm the year around, generally sleep on the floor in any case.

On the last day, when all the bandages had been taken off, Baba gave Dr. Modi *dhotis* to be distributed to the men, and He gave saris to me for the women. Most of the patients didn't want to leave, saying that they had never before been given so much attention and loving care. At night all of us helpers were given a dinner during which Baba produced a watch for Dr. Modi that was working and showing the exact time, although it was taken from the air. The Doctor confessed to me the following day that he couldn't sleep the whole night, being unable to understand how such a thing was possible.

I would like to mention a small incident illustrating Bhagawan's keen sense of humour. When the villagers, mostly old, half-blinded people, came into the big shed for Dr. Modi's examination, one of the over-zealous woman volunteers agitatedly brought to Baba's attention the fact that the men and women were sitting down together instead of separately as was the custom at Prasanthi Nilayam.

"Doesn't matter, let them," He said. He smiled and added "they can't see the difference anyway!"

Ten days after Prasanthi Nilayam had been turned into an improvised hospital it was once again the scene of Maha Shivaratri. About fifty thousand people attended. The proceedings were much the same as last year. After hoisting the flag on the roof of the temple, Baba made a speech and mentioned that greed is the root of all competition in the world today. Greed for riches, for authority, for power over fellow men, etc. This should be overcome by cultivating detachment, tolerance, the spirit of service and deepening of faith in an ever-present God.

In the forenoon, He did the *abishekam* by pouring a stream of ashes over the statue of the Sai Baba of Shirdi. This time I reacted with such a flood of unexpected tears that I had to pull my sari over my head to hide my face. In the evening, before the *Lingodbhava,* the emergence of the *linga,* Baba spoke to His devotees and said:

"The *Sai bhaktas* have to be pioneers in a new revolution, a transformation of character and endeavour; they have to fill themselves with love so that the shower of unselfish universal love can scotch the flames of anger, hatred, fear and anxiety that are consuming the world today. Sometimes, despair clouds the vision and people panic about the future of this country. But, I assure you that the country will not come to harm, either through internal or external danger. For it is Bharat (*Bha* meaning Bhagawan and *Rathi* meaning attachment), the land where the people are attached to God, and whom God loves."

Soon after Shivaratri, I was on my way home with a stopover in Madras to speak on Baba at the request of Major Rayaningar, the local Samithi President.

Six weeks later I returned to India to attend the World Conference. My husband was sorry I would not be with him for my birthday on 12th May, but he let me go without making any reproaches. I went straight to Bangalore and stayed, as before, at the Mysore palace with Rani Vijaya. Brindavan, Baba's house in Whitefield, a suburb of Bangalore, was full of people who had come to attend the Conference. Amongst them were the British writer Arthur Osborne and his Polish wife Wanda.

"My husband wrote a book (*The Incredible Sai Baba*) about the Sai Baba of Shirdi, but we were both against Sathya Sai," Wanda confided to me.

"And now?" I asked her in Polish.

"Ah! It is all different now. It is impossible not to accept Him."

She told me that her husband, besides other things, was very impressed by the depth of Baba's knowledge and His insight; yet, at other times, amused that He could be like a mischievous little boy. She told me of the surprise He gave her the other day. She was writing at her desk when suddenly a candy fell onto the paper in front of her. "There was no one in the room, and I could not understand where it came from. It was Baba! He came out laughing from behind the door."

In the afternoon we all sat around the Osbornes who were telling us about their life at the Ashram of Sri Ramana Maharishi and of the last day of his life.

"At the moment of his passing away," Wanda recollected, "a big star fell out of the sky."

"Yes, yes," intercepted one of the devotees, "I know. We were with Swami outside in Prasanthi Nilayam when this happened, and He said to us "Ramana Maharishi is gone.""

"Did He really?" the Osbornes wondered.

Prior to the World Conference, a lotus-like white structure of exquisite beauty – the Dharmakshetra – was inaugurated in Bombay on 12th May 1969 in the presence of thousands of people. It was built by Baba's devotees in that area so that it could serve as an International Centre for Sai activities. I couldn't have had a better celebration of my birthday than being present at this opening.

The Conference was held on the campus of the Bharati Vidya Bhavan outside Bombay four days later. It was attended by delegates not only from all over India, but also by delegates from the five continents.

"We have met here," said Dr. V. K. Gokak, the vice-chancellor of the University of Bangalore and a great devotee of Baba, "with the common purpose of affirming the supremacy of consciousness over matter, subject over object, seer over the seen, charioteer over the chariot, and the transcendental over the trivial. So, we will not be baffled, as others are bound to be, by the Phenomenon of the Human Form which the Formless Absolute has donned."

When Baba addressed the delegates, He first spoke of this age of materialism in which the constant repetition of the name of God is the only hope man has to rise up to God, or to bring Him near. He underlined that it did not matter which name was chosen – Ishwara, Shiva, Rama, Krishna, Jesus, Allah, Jehovah, Sai or any other.

"Of what avail is it," He went on, "if you worship My name and form without cultivating My love for all, equanimity, forbearance and state of bliss? Many of you ask for a message from Me – My life is My message... Don't try to understand Me: you cannot understand My Reality... Because I move amongst you, eat like you, talk to you, you are deluded that I am but one of you; I am also deluding you by singing and playing with you and engaging Myself in activities with you. But any moment My Divinity may be revealed to you – you must be ready, prepared for that moment..."

As He continued His talk on these lines, the electric lights suddenly went out and many people, who were heard weeping when He spoke, must have been glad that it was dark. The lights came back only at the conclusion of His discourse.

"You are the fortunate ones, because this Form is amidst you, with you and before you."

At the public meeting on the closing day, I could see from the platform the magnitude of the crowd. Mr. Indulal Shah, the chief organiser of the Conference, told me that there must be at least a hundred thousand people there. When I asked Baba whether I was to speak on meditation, He thought that the crowd was too large for that. "On anything you want," He said. Since I never prepare my speeches, it made no difference to me, and by His Grace all went well.

Coming out of the guest house on the morning before His departure, I witnessed a most unusual scene. When Baba appeared in the doorway all the policemen assembled near the entrance prostrated themselves in front of Him. "Even the police!" I wondered to myself, wishing that I had a camera with me. They were on duty around the Dharmakshetra during the opening of the Conference and came to pay homage to Him.

I returned to Brindavan with Him. In the car, I asked when He planned to come to America, since He had thrice promised this to me at our very first meeting.

"But I didn't say when." After a pause He added, "in My own time... At the present there are too many swamis (holy men) in America, each known by the amount of money he charges."

"Some have not even been swamis before," I added. "I know of a small business man who decided that posing as a swami was the fastest way to make money and to gain prestige and adoration in addition."

Actually both the Americas are a fertile ground for all sorts of pseudo yogis and swamis, because people are now searching for something beyond this material world and become easy prey to such unscrupulous imposters.

I also asked Him what I should do about giving *mantras* because many people come to me for them.

"The greatest of all the mantras is *Om*," He said.

"Yes, but people want a personal one and how would I know which *mantra* to give?"

"Ask me," was his answer. And this is what I have been doing ever since.

Dr. Sam Sandweiss, formerly a scoffer and unbeliever, now turned into a most staunch and ardent devotee, recently told me that he had been with Baba when a young man asked Him about his mantra.

"You have a very good one," Sai assured him, "I gave it to you."

"No, I got it from Mataji Indra Devi."

"I am giving them through her," he assured the young man. Hearing this reassured me, too.

MORE MIRACLES

Those days in Brindavan life was totally different from that at Prasanthi Nilayam, which is an Ashram and has fixed times for the *Omkar* (the repetition of *Om* twenty-one times), which is done at five in the morning, for *bhajans*, meditation, selection of people for the interviews and for Baba's *Darshan*. Brindavan, on the other hand, is His summer residence where He stays sometimes and extends hospitality to people accompanying Him. In most cases, we sleep on the floor and roll up or tuck away our beddings for the daytime. Since there are no scheduled activities, everyone is left to do what he or she pleases, which usually consists in trying to catch a glimpse of Baba when He comes downstairs from His room to have His meal or to see the devotees gathered outside in the vast garden. He is generally very busy and has to attend to countless other things – from planning the Summer Course for students all over India and building colleges, to attending to the various needs of His devotees. In spite of certain discomforts, even those accustomed to living in palaces or luxurious homes deem it a great privilege and joy to stay there.

Once, when an old devotee was saying her prayers sitting on the bed (the only place where one could sit in the room) and uttering "Bhagawan" from time to time, He happened to hear it while passing by.

"Did you call me?" He asked quietly coming into the room.

"Oh! Oh!" exclaimed the old lady, frightened by His unexpected appearance, while the rest of us couldn't help laughing at His *leela*.

He is that way, playful as a child at times, serious as a wise scholar the next moment, but always as kind and tender as a loving mother. He can also be awe-inspiring like thunder and lightning. But He is God-like at all times.

Once, when passing through another room, He noticed someone's *japa-mala* on the window sill. Picking it up, He quickly sat down in the armchair and stretching out his right arm, pretended to do the *japa* (telling beads on a rosary). Then, turning His head to an imaginary person, asked *"Dhobi aya?"* (Did the laundry man come?), and quickly went back to the beads. We laughed, but He remarked that this is the way many people pray – showing off their piousness whereas in reality their minds are preoccupied by trivial matters.

The omnipresence, omnipotence and omniscience of Sai Baba are too evident to be disputed, even by those who do not accept Him. There are several instances confirming this, some of which I have already related. I remember Dr. Bhagawantham telling me how, when he was present at *Shivaratri* for the first time, he saw Baba produce a jewel and then affix it to the forehead of the silver statue of the Sai Baba of *Shirdi*. He kept wondering how the jewel could stay on a metal surface without falling off. During the evening discourse, Baba brought up this fact, saying that a certain person in the audience was puzzled that the jewel didn't fall off the statue. "Why," He asked, "didn't this person think that if I could produce the jewel, I could also make it stick?"

Kamala, one of my Indian students in Mexico, told me that she went to Prasanthi Nilayam during their home leave. At the interview Baba told her not to worry so much about her son, adding that he had just saved the boy's life. She was puzzled. Returning to her family, she learned that her son was almost killed by a shot-put while standing on the sports field. At the moment when the metal ball was about to strike his head, someone pushed him aside and the ball landed on his foot.

According to witnesses, however, the boy was standing all alone and there was no one near him. He, however, insisted that he had not moved himself, but that somebody pushed him. After hearing his mother's account of her meeting with Sai Baba, the boy's heart was filled with gratitude. His faith was strengthened still more after he saw Baba cure his paralysed friend.

My very dear friend and a staunch devotee, Robert Silver, a lawyer in Ventura, California, once brought Dr. Benito Reyes and his wife, Dominga, to Tecate from Manila. They had come to California to establish a school along spiritual lines. I showed them a film on Bhagawan during which Mrs. Reyes suddenly saw His face change into that of Jesus. At first she thought it was an illusion, but then it changed again into the face of her own Master and she heard him say: "Could you not recognise me in any other form?" Tears came to her eyes and she couldn't stop crying.

It wasn't long before she and her husband went to India to see Baba. There Dr. Reyes, whose great wish was to receive a ring from Baba, mentally addressed Him saying: "Baba, could you please give me a little ring? I will never voice my request, but I am asking you now with my mind." During the interview, Bhagawan, after producing a ring, told Dr. Reyes: "You were asking for a ring, now you've got it. Whenever you want to ask me anything, you need only ask it in your mind: I will receive your prayer." Baba showered a great deal of love and grace on the couple during their stay. As they were returning home, Dr. Reyes wished that he had some ash too. When they entered their house – which had been locked during their absence – they found it full of black ash! Every room, even the kitchen, was covered by it and it took them quite a while to clean it up. "Baba's *leela*," someone remarked, "shows one shouldn't be too greedy."

In Bombay, my friend Mrs. Shakuntala Amersey told me of an incident concerning her driver Rao. Rao had a physically disabled, deaf and dumb son, Balu, who lived with his mother in their village. When Shakuntala went to Prasanthi Nilayam, Rao was also called in for an interview. Baba told him all about his boy and gave some *vibhuti* for him. Later, when Bhagawan was expected in Bombay, the driver brought Balu to town hoping that Baba would cure him. But as His visit was postponed, Rao left Balu with his daughter in one of the suburbs as the boy could not look after himself. One afternoon, Balu disappeared from his sister's house while everyone was resting. A search party of about forty people combed the neighbourhood, but they could not find him. The father was grief stricken and feared that the poor boy had been run over by a car. He handed two letters to Bhagawan asking for help and also wrote a third one, but had no chance to give it to Him.

The day Baba was expected at Shakuntala's house, preparations were being made to receive Him. That morning Balu was discovered sitting outside the gates of the house. Rao's joy knew no bounds, but he failed to understand how his deaf and dumb son could have got there after an absence of twenty-six days, looking well fed and content. The watchman from across the street said that he saw a car dropping the boy at the gate and driving away.

When Bhagawan arrived in the evening, He went straight to Balu, who at once prostrated himself before Him. Addressing Rao, Baba said: "Writing me three letters, eh? Are you happy now?" He knew of the third letter even though it had not been handed over to Him.

It is said that a person can go to see Baba only if he is called. Don Heath of San Francisco had been planning to travel overland from Europe and go to Prasanthi Nilayam. One evening, wanting to show Baba's photo to his friends, he reached for his wallet. It was missing along with Baba's photo and the money he had saved for the trip. Closing his eyes and trying to remember where he could have left it, he saw a vision of Bhagawan shaking His head, as if saying "no." Don realised that Baba didn't want him to come just yet.

Six months later some of Don's friends were preparing to go to India and invited him to join them. "If Baba is omnipotent and if He wants me to come now, let Him give me a sign so that I might know that the time is right," said Don to himself. The very next day he received a card from the post office asking him to pick up an undelivered package. It was his wallet with all the money and Baba's photo in it! Since then Don has made several trips to see Bhagawan and is now running the Sai Baba Centre in San Francisco.

Bhagawan has also answered many of my S.O.S. calls, sometimes rescuing me before I was even aware of the forthcoming danger. For example, one rainy day the windshield wiper of my car seemed to be torn off by a forceful hand, forcing me to stop at a petrol station to get a new one. The attendant there discovered a big nail in my tyre. Had it not been discovered and removed, I would probably have had a fatal accident since I was driving at a very high speed.

On another occasion, on a stormy night, my car skidded on the wet asphalt of a three lane freeway. It made two and a half turns from one side to the other, without resulting in any accident.

"What about the cars passing on both sides in opposite directions?" asked the policeman of the patrol car which later passed by.

"They were passing on both sides and I was between them," I answered.

"You must be having a very special guardian angel," the surprised officer remarked.

"A very special one," I admitted, without mentioning, however, anything about Bhagawan or his protective ring.

There were several dramatic incidents which happened on our ranch in Tecate, of which I shall mention only two. One took place on a day when non-stop rain flooded the entire ground floor, turning the entrance hall, library, lecture hall and meditation room into a veritable lake. There was nothing one could do as long as it continued to pour.

"Bhagawan," I said, directing my plea to His picture, "You who can do everything, please stop this rain." In a few minutes, the steady downpour suddenly stopped and everyone, including our luncheon guests, helped the servants drain out the water.

"If Sai Baba could stop the rain," said one of the guests when everything was over, "couldn't He also pump out the water?"

"Oh! No! That was our job, He did His," I replied remembering Baba saying that individual effort and Divine grace are both interdependent, that without effort there will be no conferment of grace.

On another occasion, a big fire broke out on our ranch on the day following the graduation ceremony of our annual July Teacher's Course. Returning from a drive, I was taken aback by the sight of a wall of flames rapidly approaching the Students' House and threatening to consume it in a matter of minutes.

"Did you talk to Sai Baba?" asked my husband.

"I am going to," I answered.

"Ask Him to change the direction of the wind," someone called after me.

Lighting all the candles in Baba's meditation room I said aloud: "Bhagawan, I am not asking You for anything, just letting you know about the fire. If you think that the house serves a purpose and should remain, You will protect it. Otherwise let it burn down, whatever you decide is all right with me."

On coming out I saw the flames 'running' in another direction, away from the house and towards the mountain, where the American firemen stopped them in time. Rosita, my adopted Mexican daughter, who was watching the fire together with Lynn Poulton, one of our students, told me afterwards that both of them distinctly felt Baba's presence. She also 'saw' His hand make a sweeping movement after which the entire line of the oncoming flames changed direction. "Un verdadero milagro, (a real miracle) señora," the workers kept repeating in amazement.

This was the second big fire we had had within a few years. During the first one, the entire mountain was in flames and at 'Sai Nilayam' – our ranch on the American side – a tent and a car were burnt down and all the big trees around the house scorched. When the devotees returned from the top of Cuchuma, where they were trapped for several hours and prayed desperately for help, everyone was surprised to find the house untouched. The only trouble was the black soot which had fallen all over, with the exception of the meditation room. There was not the slightest trace of it there, even the carpet in front of Baba's picture remained spotlessly white.

But of all the miracles of Bhagawan the greatest, in my opinion, is the change which He produces in human beings. Cynics, scoffers and rowdies turn into His devoted followers without a trace of their former habits and behaviour.

Joel Reardon – a film producer, director and writer – says about himself that he was a typical Hollywood product, without any beliefs or religion.

When his wife, Diana, returned from India with photos of Baba, he protested vehemently at them being displayed in their home, and kept referring to Sai as 'this *character*.'

The Reardons were on the brink of a divorce when, a year later, Diana's mother was again going to Prasanthi Nilayam and invited her daughter to join her. Joel also decided to come along with the purpose of exposing 'this *character*.' He intended to ask Him for something no human being can give: a rainbow.

Shocked by the primitivity of the room allotted to them, he thought of returning to Bangalore, but the taxi had already left. Since smoking is prohibited in the Ashram, Diana took him outside to the hills. Sitting there on a rock he suddenly saw a big rainbow rise out of the ground and stand straight in front of him. Flabbergasted, he called everyone's attention to it. After a few minutes the rainbow disappeared bit by bit, starting from its top. Regaining his composure, Joel began to speculate on the possibility of what he had seen to be a reflection of a rainbow somewhere in the distance, although the blue skies were sunny and cloudless.

The next morning, when they were called into the interview room, Bhagawan went straight up to Joel and asked: "Well, *character*, how did you like your rainbow?" and leaving him speechless, turned to talk to others in the room.

Coming back to his senses and still not believing what had happened, Joel decided that when his turn came, he would ask this time for a fruit out of season, a fig.

Instantly, Bhagawan produced the wished fruit, and giving half of it to a sick lady, for a cure, He put the other half into the hand of Reardon's little daughter, saying: "Are you satisfied now?"

He was, I dare say, because he cut off his ties with Hollywood and went to live with his family in close proximity of Bhagawan.

BABA'S BIRTHDAY

That particular year (1969) I had not planned to go for Baba's birthday, as I was due to visit India a little later. All the same, one evening after meditation, looking at His picture, I found myself saying: "Bhagawan, take me to Puttaparthi for Your birthday." Two days later, I received a phone call from Chuck Wein, a young man who used to come to our Sai Baba Centre in Los Angeles. He was calling from the Warner Brothers motion picture studio.

"Mataji, can you go to India tomorrow? Warner Brothers will pay your passage if you will go to ask Sai Baba's permission to make a documentary film of His life..." Somehow, I wasn't even surprised and answered very calmly: "Tomorrow is Sunday and all the offices are closed, but I can leave on Tuesday."

"Who is paying for my ticket?" I asked the Air India manager in Los Angeles.

"Warner Brothers," he replied.

I arrived just in time for the celebrations which began early in the morning when Bhagawan hoisted the Prasanthi Nilayam flag on the roof of the temple. He then declared that He was *Shiva-Shakti*[1] incarnated in human form, in order to lead men towards God. He exhorted people to cleanse and purify their hearts, to make *viveka* (discrimination) their flag post, unfurl the flag of love on it and let it flutter joyfully in the wind of grace. He also said that He is born in each of us as love.

"Only that day, when love is born in you, can it be My birthday."

At eleven o'clock, Swami went from the Temple to the auditorium in procession. His mother, Eswaramma, started the ceremony by first garlanding Sai, then annointing His head with a flower dipped into a cup of fragrant oil. She was followed by several others chosen by Baba from among His old devotees. The procession then moved, headed by the Temple elephant Sai Gita.

Later in the afternoon, at the meeting of the Sathya Sai Seva Samithis in the interview room, Bhagawan listened to the first three proposals about the finances and then advised:

"No banking, no soliciting money from the public, no fancy offices. When a need for funds arises, the Samithi members get together and each person, one by one, puts his contribution into a basket kept in a separate room, so that the man who gave, say, one hundred rupees should not feel superior to the one who gave ten. If the need for funds is greater than the sum collected, let me know. Don't make a business out of it all: it will kill the spiritual aim of the Samithis. This is what has happened to most churches and religious organisations. They started out with high ideals and ended up with a big business... When I come to visit your towns, do not make any elaborate arrangements: all that is needed is a platform, a microphone, voices to sing *bhajans* and, above all, genuine devotion."

The day before I was ready to return home, Bhagawan called me in to give His blessings. At parting He produced, with the familiar circling motion of His hand, a beautiful golden medallion of the Goddess Lakshmi.

"I don't want anything, Bhagawan," I pleaded.

"This is not for you... for the protection of the house: no more fires."

I did not know at that moment how badly we would need His protection a few months later when we were about to loose the ranch.

After returning from India, I went to the Warner Brothers Studio, but not a soul there had ever heard of Sai Baba let alone my trip to Him!

"Another *leela* of Baba?" wondered Dick Bock when I told him about it.

After a whole year's interval I made another trip to Prasanthi Nilayam. The All India Conference of Sri Sathya Sai Seva Samithis was taking place there just before the birthday celebrations. One of the Beatles, John Lennon, arrived suddenly with his wife Yoko and another couple. Incidentally, I kept calling him Mr. Lemon until he corrected me. Whenever I relate this incident everyone is amused at my ignorance, but since I don't go to the movies or watch TV, I had only a vague idea of the Beatles but didn't know their proper names. Unfortunately, they left disappointed because they were not able to meet Baba: they just saw Him at a distance.

The morning of the birthday, I was to have hung a picture of Krishna in the room where Baba takes His meals. To my dismay I discovered that the painting was locked in one of the guest rooms. In vain I tried to find someone who would open it, but everyone had already left for the ceremony. Not finding anyone, I searched despairingly for an iron pipe with which I could pry open the back door. Running back again to the kitchen door I suddenly noticed an iron pipe lying nearby. "Bhagawan!" I exclaimed thankfully, not having the time to figure out how it had got there.

I was upstairs with the picture just a few moments before Bhagawan came in. After we wished Him a happy birthday, He told me also to participate in the annointment ceremony, a great honour and privilege for which I was grateful.

At the end of the ceremony he extracted Himself from the mountain of garlands, and walked towards Elsa Anderson, who was sitting on a chair near the wall. She had a cancerous hip bone, and was put into the Prasanthi Nilayam hospital the moment she arrived. To relieve the agony, Baba gave her some *vibhuti* and said that she would be better in three days. Sure enough she was able to sit up and attend the ceremonies. Bhagawan came close to her and commanded her to get up and walk. "Oh, I couldn't do that," she said, but He took her hand and she walked away with Him to the loud cheering of the crowd.

Two days later, Elsa now well and happy, was leaving together with her husband and Dick Bock. Dick had come only for the purpose of making a record of Baba's *bhajans*, but was leaving as an ardent devotee. As I was planning to drive along with them, we were all called for a parting interview. At the end of it when He asked his usual question "What do you want?," I silently opened the empty silver box of *vibhuti* which He had given me in Bombay.

"I shall now give you real *akshaya patra*." With these words, He made several circles in the air with His hand but it was empty. Then He raised both arms, and when He lowered them to chest level, a *kamandulu*[2] suddenly appeared between His cupped palms. Unscrewing it, He started pouring the fragrant *vibhuti* onto a sheet of paper which someone had quickly spread on the floor. After the container was emptied, He began twirling His finger inside it causing a flow of *vibhuti* to fall on the paper. We all watched this *leela* with amazement, never having seen anything like it before. We poured the *vibhuti* back into the *kamandulu*, but twice as much was still on the paper. Bhagawan then touched the container saying "It will never be empty." Over come by joy I almost forget to thank Him for His grace.

"If the supply is inexhaustible, can I give it to everybody?" I asked eagerly.

"No. Use it only for healing," He instructed.

I decided to stay on, and so the Andersons and Dick left without me. In the evening Baba asked me to speak before His discourse. I proposed to the listeners that to show our devotion and love for Him we should do something worthy of Him, instead of just using high-sounding words. The audience accepted my suggestion to remain silent for a few minutes and resolve individually what each one would do to be more compassionate, more loving, more considerate to other human beings and animals and to be a better devotee. After a few moments of silence I chanted *Om Shanti, Shanti, Shanti*, in which they all joined. I then touched His feet with a heart full of gratitude, love and devotion.

After the birthday celebrations were over, Baba sent me to lecture in Sri Lanka, where the *bhaktas* were eagerly awaiting His message. From Colombo I went to Jaffna, where many of Baba's photos along the wall of the worship room were covered with *vibhuti*. My host was Dr. Somasundaram.

Upon returning from Sri Lanka, Baba took me with Him to Goa, where all of us stayed as guests of his staunch devotees, Lt. Governor Dr. Nakul Sen, a great scholar, and his wife Indu, a woman of rare qualities. Baba was received with military honours, salutes, guards and the ringing of bells from the church tower: Goa had been under Portuguese domination and many people there are Christians. The big mansion was beautifully illuminated and decorated with flowers and green leaves.

The next day Bhagawan didn't feel well. The doctors diagnosed it as a severe attack of appendicitis and advised an immediate operation. Anxiety, sadness and tears were evident on almost everybody's face. In the meditation room, instead of praying, I ended up arguing with His photos about the operation. The five doctors were beside themselves when Baba ordered public *bhajans* and a meeting to be arranged two days later. "He will never be able to attend them," the physicians declared. The day came, everyone nervously watched the time, but exactly at six o'clock the door opened and Baba came in as radiant as the shining sun and took His seat. "Doctor," I said to one of them afterwards, "you forgot that He is not just a patient, but Bhagawan."

Before I left to get home for Christmas, He gave me a little medallion with Himself on one side and Nataraj[3] on the other.

"Christmas present," He said.

When I arrived in New York, where I was to speak the same night to Hilda Charlton's group of young people, I realised I wouldn't be able to make it. The plane was two hours late, two other planes had just landed, and the queue for Customs was the longest I had ever seen. I turned my thoughts to Baba and said: "Bhagawan, if you want me to be with your devotees tonight, please do some thing about it." No sooner had I made this silent appeal that a man in uniform came up to me, asked for my disembarkation card, signed it and, showing me the exit, disappeared again into the crowd. For a moment I stood still, not quite believing what had happened. The devotees who were meeting me said they were about to leave, thinking that I must have missed the plane.

End Notes:
1. The combined Masculine and Feminine Principles of Divinity.
2. A small receptacle usually made of brass.
3. Aspect of Shiva doing the Tandava dance.

BABA IS WITH ME ALL THE TIME

During one of my trips to Bhagawan (I have made nineteen of them so far) I had landed in Delhi where my hostess, Maharani Prithwi of Jind, informed me that He was away touring some villages, but no one knew exactly where. Surmounting all sorts of obstacles, I finally caught up with Him in Dharwar, where He had arrived to spend the night at the house of Dr. Adke, Vice-chancellor of Karnataka University. All the men accompanying Baba looked more dead than alive, only He looked fresh and cheerful without a trace of fatigue.

"Indra Devi!" He stopped in surprise, not expecting to see me there.

The following day was supposed to be a day of rest before continuing the tour, but Baba kept seeing all the people who had crowded the entire garden.

The next morning we started out for the last five villages scheduled on the tour. Holding garlands, coconuts and burning lamps, the villagers stood for hours in the hot sun all along the road, waiting for Bhagawan's car to pass, in the hope of catching a glimpse of Him. Bhagawan would raise His hand to bless them though the window, sometimes even getting out of the car to let them have a closer *Darshan*. They would then touch His feet or the hem of His robe. In some places the human wall was so dense that our cars could hardly get by.

On the way back to Brindavan, He suddenly commanded "Sing something."

"Bhagawan, You are not addressing me by any chance, for I cannot sing. I never could." But He was so insistent that I had to give in and painfully go through one of my favourite *bhajans*, all the while wishing I could sink through the floor.

"Indra Devi can sing *bhajans* very nicely," Baba announced the following morning at breakfast.

"Oh! Please, Bhagawan, don't You spread this kind of rumour," I begged. Strangely enough, ever since that day, I actually can sing – only *bhajans*, however. This was the greatest surprise I brought home for my husband, my mother and all those who knew about my total inability to carry a tune.

A few weeks before Shivarathri, 1972, I was back in India again. Baba remained in Bangalore because construction work was in progress in Prasanthi Nilayam, and the festival could not be celebrated there. I was disappointed to miss it, especially the *abishekam* which so greatly affected me the last two times I saw it. The morning before Shivarathri I needed some of the healing *vibhuti* which Baba had given me four years earlier. The supply had gone down to half and stayed that way, no matter how much I gave to those who needed it. Unscrewing the lid I uttered a cry of surprise: the container was full. Thanking Him for this later on, I said that I found the *kamandulu* 'full to the brim.'

"Not to the brim," He corrected, "it was only full."

During His stay I told Him how 'Sai Yoga' originated, and asked for His permission to use that name. He then enquired whether I could teach it to the students at the Summer Course which he was inaugurating in May. Making a quick trip home I was back six weeks later happy to be able to introduce Sai Yoga at Bhagawan's first Summer Course on Indian Culture and Spirituality. I continued to teach it the following two seasons.

The Summer Course was held in a big shed of palm leaves and bamboo constructed at the back of Bhagawan's house. It served as a classroom for about 800 people. Tuition, board and lodging were all provided free by Him, and He Himself gave discourses every evening at six O'clock, after the last *bhajans* were over. The day usually started with the Sai Yoga class and meditation which I conducted from 6.30 a.m. to 8 a.m. Other classes were held from 9 a.m. to 12 noon and from 3 p.m. to 5 p.m.

It is difficult to put into words the impact this course had on the boys and girls who attended it. Many came reluctantly, forced by their parents to attend, but after the course they were so completely changed that they were deeply grateful for the experience.

The following year, during the Summer Course, two incidents took place which were also reported in the *News Chronicle* of Ludhiana of 20th July 1973. Three boys had slipped away from camp one night after dark. They had a few drinks, ate meat and went to a cinema. Coming back quietly in the early hours they felt happy that their escapade had gone unnoticed. When Baba came in the next morning He mentioned that incident saying that they could probably deceive the world but not Him. He then described the incident in detail and asked the boys to stand up voluntarily before He named them. Hanging their heads in shame they stood up.

Another student who was a chain smoker had promised Baba several times to break this bad habit. One day when he came into the classroom after smoking behind the cowshed, Baba pointed to him saying that he had just broken his promise, which the boy denied. To everyone's surprise Baba then materialised a photo showing the boy smoking his cigarette in the exact place where he had been. Faced with this, the boy pledged never to smoke again.

BABA'S GRACE
FOR HUSBAND AND MOTHER

In March 1972, while passing through Bombay, I had my life reading done from the *Bhrigu Samhita* (Book of Bhrigu) by Chayashastri Kantilal Pandya.

Amongst other things which proved to be correct, he read the following: "During 1966-67 you came in contact with a Maha Purusha due to merits of past lives." Then interrupting himself he explained, "Maha Purusha means God," and continued: "By coming in contact with Him the little *maya* (illusion) that was still there has left you. Your husband will also come under the shadow of your guru, the Maha Purusha."

This was the only statement which I doubted, because I knew that my husband being a Christian and also very involved in Anthroposophy, would never come to Sai Baba.

However, the impossible happened when after a grave illness, his recovery was very slow, and we, together with Rosita, came to India in spite of all predictions that he would not survive the journey. But with Bhagawan in my heart I had no doubts or fears.

The love and attention with which He surrounded my husband, and the treatment He gave him soon put my husband back on his feet. First Sai produced, one by one, from His fingertips, 33 pills which were to be taken daily. Then, a few days later, in Bombay, he treated my husband by rubbing him with a fragrant oil that exuded from His upturned palm. I could hardly believe my eyes when I saw Svetik attempting to touch Bhagawan's feet, but He gently prevented it. The next day my husband was well enough to travel alone to Europe where I was to join him in two weeks.

Since we had arrived just after Shivaratri, I had no chance to see the *linga* Bhagawan produced, but was told that it was a very unusual one. It kept changing colours all the time and had a little light shining inside it. Someone suggested that I ask Baba to show it to me since He had not given it to anyone. One morning, when He entered the guest-room of the Dharmakshetra with photos of the *lingam*, I asked where it was now. "Gone back to its place," He answered giving each one of us a photo of it.

I was told that three years earlier He had produced a *lingam* similar to this one but a little smaller; also it was not incandescent nor did it change colours. According to Sai the *lingam* was so pure that it should not be touched. The whole night it remained on the flower-covered tray where Bhagawan had placed it. In the morning a Brahmin was to take it to the Temple before bringing it to Baba. Unable to withstand the temptation to have a closer look at it, the priest reached out to pick it up and the moment his hand touched the *lingam* it vanished. Terrified the Brahmin stood there until Bhagawan called for him and asked what had caused the *lingam* to appear at His feet in the room upstairs. The trembling priest fell on his knees and confessed his mistake to be forgiven.

Before returning to Prasanthi Nilayam, Baba was going to visit Sandur and included me in His party. He had promised the Maharaj[1] (King) that he would lay the foundation stone for his new Ferro-silicone Plant. While there, Baba also inaugurated a public park, visited the Iron Factory, the school and addressed three packed public meetings. He visited three temples too, and the priests of each of them prostrated themselves at His feet and bestowed on Him those honours usually accorded only to the images of deities.

The Maharaja turned his beautiful palace into a fairy tale pageant to receive the 'King of Kings.' It was an unforgettable and unique experience for all of us who accompanied Baba on this trip.

On the way back I was surprised to learn that Bhagawan seemed to have suddenly turned against me and had accused me of things I had neither said nor done. I was at a loss to find an explanation for this drastic change, and had no chance to clear up the matter as He was avoiding me after we reached Bangalore. The best I could do under the circumstances was to speed up my departure.

Arriving in San Diego, my husband, Rosita and I drove straight from the airport to the nursing home to see my mother. I remained with her, as it was evident that she would not last long. Early the following morning she passed away peacefully; I would never have forgiven myself if I had come too late. Only then did I realise why Bhagawan had wanted me to go home earlier and had made me understand it in His own way, which was also a test of my faith in Him.

I have found that when I am away from Bhagawan I don't even miss Him any longer, because He is so much within me. I suppose that this is probably the reason why I never 'see' or 'hear' Him, as so many others did, even those who have never met Him in His physical form. It is just the way I cannot see my heart although I know it is there. I feel He is with me all the time, guarding, teaching and guiding me step by step.

"That is right," He confirmed, when I told Him about it once, "step by step."

End Notes:
1. The Maharaja, like all other Indian princes, has been stripped of his political power. He is still revered by his former subjects and provides work for 3,000 people in his Sandur Pig Iron Factory.

SAI YOGA

SAI YOGA
INTRODUCTION

The practice of Sai Yoga may bring about a complete change in your life, especially if your attitude has been negative, pessimistic or cynical towards your family, friends, or life in general. It will show you the way out of the cobwebs of irrational likes and dislikes, release you from the rat race you may be caught up in, and open a new chapter in your life. I hope it will be a totally new and different experience for you, even if you have been doing the *asanas* before.

The practice of Sai Yoga will be much more effective, however, if someone reads the instructions aloud while you are assuming the *asanas*. The reading should be very slow and every word should be 'felt' by the reader, and pronounced in a flowing way as if accompanied by music. If this is not possible, then first read them yourself while mentally assuming the posture, in order to merge into it, to integrate with it, so that when you actually get into the posture, you 're-live' the words you have been reading. Add, if you wish, your own thoughts along the same lines. In our classes we always chant *Om* aloud after each *asana*. You may, however, wish to do so silently.

If you are a newcomer to Yoga, you must first learn the proper deep breathing technique. Then you should learn the Yoga postures thoroughly. Both these are given in the pages following. Only after you know these perfectly should you begin on Sai Yoga. This is essential because in Sai Yoga you should not consciously think about the position of your body, hands and feet while you are performing the *asanas*, but concentrate upon the thoughts which accompany the postures.

Every *asana* can be done in three different ways, although outwardly it will look the same. In the first instance, you merely breathe in, assume the posture holding the breath, then release it while breathing out. In the second instance you imagine the *prana* (vital cosmic energy) and healing forces flowing to that part of your body or to that particular organ which is affected by the *asana*. In the third instance, you turn your thoughts to the spiritual aspect of your being and think of the Eternal Great Light which you also carry in your heart as a divine spark.

General Rules and Regulations

Before starting on Sai Yoga, you must already be able to assume the *asanas* without any trouble, and as correctly as possible, since in Sai Yoga you do not concentrate any longer on the proper way of doing the *asana*, because your mind must be turned towards a spiritual experience.

That is why in assuming, let us say the Cobra Posture, it should be understood that you have to keep the feet and heels together and the elbows bent, fingertips at shoulder level, the lower part of the abdomen on the floor and the head thrown backwards. In short, the posture must be done correctly. The same applies to every other *asana*, except, of course, if you are unable to touch your feet in the Stretching posture or to properly assume the *Yoga Mudra*, etc. If such is the case, you do it to the best of your ability, or assume any of the preparatory or easy versions of the given *asana*.

The same general rules and regulations which are observed when practising yoga *asanas* are to be observed in Sai Yoga:
1. Always practise the *asanas* on an empty stomach.
2. Practise them in a well-ventilated room.
3. All *asanas* should be coupled with deep breathing done with a closed mouth, except when contraindicated.

4. Practise the *asanas* for not less than 15 minutes and not longer than an hour. This, of course, does not apply to an advanced student of Yoga.
5. Relax frequently between postures.
6. Use a folded blanket or a pad to sit or lie on. It should be about an inch thick unless your vertebrae are extremely sensitive. For doing the Headstand you can double the pad.
7. If the top of your head is very tender and doing the Headstand becomes painful, cut out a foam rubber doughnut-shaped ring and place it on the floor to put your head on. This will minimise the pressure on the crown of the head.
8. Wear comfortable, loose and clean clothing while practising the *asanas*.
9. After a prolonged illness, begin practising the *asanas* very slowly, for not more than 15 minutes. Do a few breathing exercises and only one or two easy *asanas*, gradually increasing the number as you regain your strength. Relax after every posture.

A serious student of Yoga should abstain from the use of meat, alcohol, tobacco, drugs and other stimulants and lead a clean, meaningful life, spending time in meditation, contemplation, reading of good books, keeping company with people who have higher goals in life and whose habits are not base, vulgar and dirty.

Deep Breathing

It takes a few minutes to teach a person Deep Breathing, but to explain it in writing is not so simple. To make it easier, let us start in a rather unconventional way.

Lie down on a mat or carpet. Stretch both your arms above your head, then drop them alongside and relax. Now pretend that you are gradually falling asleep. You then begin to breath with a different sound, because you have slightly tightened the glottis. You will also notice that the effort of drawing in the air while inhaling is felt in the throat rather than in the nostrils.

Do not move your shoulders or heave the chest, but let your lungs and ribs slowly expand sideways as the air begins to enter them. Continue doing this breathing still pretending that you are asleep.

It may help you to imagine that you are on a beach, watching the waves of the ocean. With every mounting wave you inhale, and with every receding wave you exhale. This should make your breathing even and rhythmic; if you strain, it will turn into snoring.

Now, 'wake up' and begin yawning and stretching, slowly sit up and get on your feet. Stand straight, keeping your spine erect, without tension. Close your eyes and begin doing the deep breathing again, slowly filling the lower part of the lungs with air, then the middle and then the upper part. Don't, however, raise or move your chest or stiffen your body. The breathing in and out should resemble the movements of an expanding and contracting accordion, that is sideways, not up and down.

To start, don't take more than five or six deep breaths at a time or you may get dizzy. However, you can repeat the exercise later in the day again. Gradually increasing the number of breaths, you can eventually bring it to sixty a day, which should be the limit for an average person. This differs of course in the case of yogis or even advanced students.

Every Yoga posture is done with the Deep Breathing as are the breathing exercises, except when otherwise instructed; in which case, follow instructions.

On the Om

Om is the true symbol of God. The literal translation from Sanskrit of this great mantra is 'instrument of thought'. It signifies the ideal inaudible sound from which creation, came into being. When recited properly, this word is the indicator of the Divine power and produces great harmony in the body and mind.

In Sanskrit there is a special symbol for this sacred sound: In English it is made up phonetically of three letters: A, U and M. The two vowels 'A' and 'U' blend into "O". The 'm' is sounded without parting the lips.

Repeat this sound, not in order to form a habit, but with thought upon its meaning, the understanding of the nature of individual consciousness and to attain higher contemplation. It is recited by Hindus at the beginning and end of all prayers, hymns and words of worship. During the Summer Course on Spirituality and Indian Culture held for college students in Brindavan in May 1972, Sai Baba spoke on the Om in one of His daily discourses:

"Om is as broad and widespread as the sky. If we can understand the aspect and real meaning of the Om then we will have understood the contents of the Shastras (sacred scriptures of the Hindus). Om is one and only one, without a second. This one sound Om is telling us it is identical with Brahman (God). This sound of Om (pranava) represents the entire content of Brahman.

"This sound Om is a combination of four elements: three sounds (A, and U, and M) and the following silence. 'A' is something which is connected with the awareness. 'U' (oo) is a somewhat subtle one and is connected with the idea. One will have to say that this is not only subtle, but has some relationship with the dream state. The 'M' sound is causal. It is connected with the cause and effect and is related in some way with deep sleep. It is only combining these three in that manner that we can get a *Darshan* of *Atma*, the soul, the divine part of the human being, and this occurs during the following silence, representing *Turiya*, 'the fourth state of consciousness.' When the sound 'A' joins the sounds 'U' and 'M', then we can get the complete sound of *Om*, vibrating in the silence. If 'A' does not join with 'U' and if 'U' does not join with 'M', we do not get the complete sound of *Om*[1] at all. In this way it is only when we are able to combine the three states, the waking state, the dream state and the deep sleep state, or combine the gross aspect, the subtle aspect and the causal aspect of the body into one, and then remain silent, do we have a chance of getting a glimpse of the Divine Soul.

"For the creation of this entire world, the main roots are sounds. If there is no sound, there is no world. If there is no sound there is no creation. The basis for the origin of sound is air, and that basis is like *Omkar*. Out of the basic sound *Omkar*[2] we get many different sounds. Those are mere transformations of the shape of *Omkar*."

In his book, *The Yogas and Other Works*, Swami Vivekananda says:

"It is out of this, the holiest of all holy words, the mother of all names and forms, the eternal AUM, that the whole universe may be supposed to have been created. The AUM is the truest sound and the symbol of all possible sounds, and there is none other like it... With the repetition of the AUM, power will manifest itself more and more. Mental and physical obstacles will begin to vanish. It will strengthen the mind and bring fresh

---

[1] For more details about the mystical sound *Om*, see the *Mandukya Upanishad*.

[2] The *Om* of the Vedas became the sacred word of *Amen* of the Christians, *Hum* of the Tibetans, *Amin* of the Moslems.

energy. Chanting of the AUM is the greatest stimulus that can be given to the spiritual aspirant... It should not be uttered very loud, but in a floating way, not with force. The effects, however, are still greater when it is done silently."

Swami Yogananda, in his book *The Autobiography of a Yogi* writes: "The whole range of creation as indicated in the AUM as respectively associated with the divine powers, symbolised by the three Gods: Brahma, Vishnu and Shiva".

Relaxation

Since this is such an important aspect of Yoga, to begin with we will learn how to relax.

Lie down on your back and stretch both arms straight up. Stretch your legs and make your entire body very tense. Then drop your arms along the sides with the palms facing upwards. Relax the entire body. Now bend your knees to your chest, put your arms around them and begin to rock from side to side... after a while straighten your legs, but imagine that you still continue rocking... you are now lying in a hammock feeling very relaxed... Above you are the green treetops and the blue sky... and as you are looking up at them, you wish you could join the clouds above, you feel your body is getting lighter and lighter... and the hammock is being detached and slowly lifted by an invisible hand... Soon you find yourself above the trees... above the roofs... and a gentle breeze is still rocking your hammock, while it goes up higher and higher... until it is suspended between two clouds.

Looking down, you see tiny dots moving to and fro, these are people hustling and bustling around... and the motor cars look like little matchboxes. From your height they all look alike: it makes no difference whether it is an old Ford or a new Cadillac...

Up here, in the spacelessness of the blue sky, you experience a sense of peace and inner freedom... And you are wondering why you were paying so much attention to, spending so much time on, things that are trivial and unimportant... while giving so little time to things that are real and lasting. And you begin to realise that you must spend some time in preparation for your future existence... after you leave this body. You can take nothing with you... your position, possessions, name, fame... you have to leave everything behind. It is up to you now, to make your future existence into an experience of heaven or hell. You should try now, in this life, to come closer to the Divine Light... which is Love... which is God... which is Truth... or whatever else you may want to call it.

So when your hammock comes down again, back to earth, you should change something in your daily life... spend part of your time in contemplation, in meditation, in communion with the Giver of Light. You will never be alone once you turn to Him, and now – still rocking to and fro – you slowly begin to come down... lower and lower, until the hammock is again firmly suspended between two trees. It felt so good to have been away... but it also feels good to be back...

And now, before getting up... start yawning and s-t-r-e-t-c-h-i-n-g... then slowly... very slowly... sit up and chant... *Om.*

The Cobra Posture - Bhujangasana

Traditional Bhujangasana

To do the Cobra Posture you lie down on your abdomen, letting your forehead touch the mat, and place your arms alongside the body, keeping the legs straight, feet together and toes pointed.

Inhale deeply while slowly raising the head, then shoulders, placing then palms on the mat on either side of your chest. The fingertips should be at the same level as the shoulders. Continue raising the chest and the upper part of the body; the lower part of the abdomen, below the navel, should remain on the mat.

Gently stretch your head back, and hold your breath in the posture for as long as you comfortably can. Be sure to keep the elbows bent and close to the body.

Begin to exhale, and at the same time slowly start lowering the body until first the chin and then the forehead touches the mat. Relax in the knee-chest position to counteract the strain on the back and then repeat the posture.

Duration: Keep the Cobra Posture for a few seconds, gradually increasing the time to a few minutes. To start with do it twice and then increase to six times.

Benefits: *The Bhujangasana* has a powerful effect on the adrenal glands, situated above the kidneys like two little caps, sending to them an added supply of blood. This *asana* also helps back-aches caused by overwork or standing for long hours. It adjusts the displacements in the vertebrae and tones up the sympathetic nervous system. Women suffering from ovarian and uterine troubles should emphasise the practice of this posture.

It also helps the development of body heat. Anyone who is troubled by gas immediately after meals will be benefited by this posture.

Caution: Be sure not to make any violent jerks when doing the back bend in the Cobra, in order not to injure a rigid muscle. Always go up slowly, like a cobra lifting itself off the ground.

Variation

Inhale a deep breath, rise into the Cobra Posture without throwing the head back. Instead, while exhaling, turn your head to the extreme right. Hold breath and the position. Then return the head to its normal position. Repeat the same to the left. Then lower the body to the mat and rest in knee-chest position, with the back rounded, to relax it after the strain of holding the *asana*.

Bhujangasana, Sai Yoga Way

Let us begin on Sai Yoga with the *Bhujangasana*, the Cobra Posture. Remember to have someone read the text aloud to you slowly and feelingly.

First lie face down on the mat, with both arms extended along the sides of your body, feet together and toes pointed. Put your cheek on the mat and close your eyes. In this position, you are glued to the ground from the head to the tip of your toes, you move only like a snake or a worm. Now let us think for a moment: isn't that what we are doing, figuratively speaking, most of the time in our daily life, where everything is centered on the material world: our family life, business life, sex life, appetites and desires?

Man has completely disconnected himself from the spiritual world and has become totally engrossed in the world of matter, which is all right for an animal but not for a human being. We seem to have forgotten that, as human beings, we are of Divine origin, that we are the children of Light and not the children of Darkness. That we are a part of the spiritual world and have a Divine spark in our hearts. We usually give so little thought to that which is eternal and Divine, spending most of our time in the pursuit of fleeting things, pleasures which are here today and gone tomorrow. Once they are over they leave us with an empty heart, mind and soul.

So, let us review our daily actions and decide right now what we will do to make a change in our lives, a change that will bring us closer to the Light. We should spend some time in contemplation, meditation or prayer. Let that inner voice, that Light within us, give us strength and confidence to lead a more meaningful and useful life.

Let the Cobra Posture serve as a symbol of this awakening... As you inhale a deep breath, imagine that you are reaching for the Light as you slowly raise your head and shoulders off the ground. Imagine that you are able to first see the green grass and the flowers around, then you try to rise higher, but you

Fig. 1 *Bhujangasana* — The Cobra Posture

cannot. This is not so, however; just make a little additional effort by placing your palms on either side of your shoulders and you will find that you can rise much higher. Throwing your head back, drink in the Light that streams down your face, reaching your heart and gradually filling your entire being.

You enjoy the possibility of being able to rise above the darkness, to shake off the cobwebs that have been surrounding you, the weights that have been dragging you down deeper and deeper into the abyss.

When you are ready to return to the original position, exhale slowly while gently lowering your body to the ground. You know now that, just as you have done in this posture, you can also rise above the greyness of the usual daily routine if you want to make an effort to do so. You don't have to feel forlorn, forgotten or lonely.

Surround yourself with Light, then bring its message to those who are still groping in the dark. Since you have seen the Light, it is your duty to share it with others, with those who need a little more love, compassion and a little more kindness from you.

There will be a day when they, too, will be able to get out of the sunless pit and be a part of the Light. Just as a crawling caterpillar becomes a beautiful butterfly, similarly man, too, can reach towering heights with the help of the Divine Power, *Om*.

Continue with these thoughts as you lie down to rest. Soon you will notice a gradual change in your interests, habits and attitudes. You will see that strength and confidence will grow within you, as you realise more and more the eternal presence of the Divine Light.

The Forward Bend - Paschimotanasana

Traditional Paschimotanasana

Sit on the mat with both legs stretched forward, feet together, toes pointed upwards and hands resting on the floor with palms down on either side of your body.

Inhale a deep breath and, while holding it, raise your arms high above your head also stretching the body. Then begin to exhale while slowly bending forward until you reach your toes or soles, which you grasp firmly. Touch the knees with your forehead if you can do so, but do not bend your knees. Should you be unable to reach the toes get hold of the ankles or calves.

Remain in this position for a few seconds, holding your breath, then slowly return to the sitting position and breathe in. Repeat it once more and relax.

Duration: Hold the posture for as long as you can stay comfortable without breathing. Do not repeat it more than two or three times to begin with. When you are able to retain the *Paschimotanasana* for a longer time, you will resume breathing while keeping that position.

Benefits: The Stretching Posture affects the abdominal region and helps against constipation, indigestion and troubles caused by an enlarged spleen. It massages the pelvic region, reduces a sagging abdomen, invigorates sluggish bowels and tautens sciatic nerves and hamstring muscles. It gives vitality and energy, and also strengthens the muscles of the legs.

Caution: People who suffer from constipation should be careful in practising this *asana*, and should avoid any jerky movements while bending forward or returning to the sitting position.

Preparatory Exercise

If the Stretching Posture does not come easily to you, try the following preparatory exercises.

Sit with both legs stretched forward, then bend your right knee and get hold of the toes with your right hand. Inhale a deep breath and, while exhaling, straighten the knee and place it on the floor. Repeat this with the left leg. Then do it with both legs, stretching the legs by gliding the heels forward while still holding the toes with your hands. You will be surprised how much easier the Stretching Posture will seem to you after practising this preliminary exercise.

Paschimotanasana, Sai Yoga Way

Sit up straight, with legs extended and palms on the floor on the both sides of the body. Close your eyes, slowly take a few deep breaths and think of yourself as already having made some progress, already a step further on the path of Light. You have been able, at least to some extent, to rise above the petty

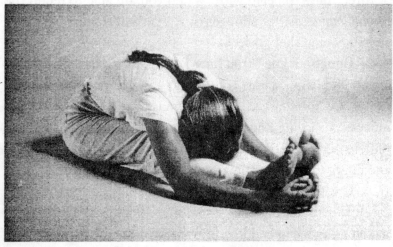

Fig. 2 *Paschimotanansaa* — The Streching Posture

things in your life: envy, spitefulness, malice, gossip and quarrels.

But there is still a part of you that is glued to the earth, that gets you down. You want to pull your entire being out of the darkness. You want to bathe in the Light, even your feet, which are always touching the darkness of the ground, seldom, if ever, seeing the Light.

So, now, inhale a deep breath, then stretch your arms above your head, imagining the Light streaming down from your fingertips, over your hands and arms, permeating your entire being; then slowly exhale, while bending forward to touch your feet. Thus you bring the Light flowing from your fingertips down to your toes and let it circulate through your whole being. Your hands will not get stained from touching your feet, just as you will not get contaminated when trying to help someone low down with a kind word, action or thought.

When the Light in your heart is shining brightly, you do not need to be afraid of coming close to those still in darkness. When you keep this circle of Light glowing inside you, you will find that you cannot be pulled down so easily into your old habits and thoughts. Eventually, you will be able to completely conquer your weakness and temptation, to free yourself from low, unworthy desires.

Always remember to bring the Light into any situation, no matter how dark it may seem. You will eventually be able to open the door to the right path flooded with Divine Light.

Remain in this *asana* for as long as you can, adding your *own* thoughts to what has been said and, then, slowly sit up and chant *Om*.

The Twist Posture - Ardha Matsyendrasana

Traditional Matsyendrasana

First Stage: Sit on the floor with both legs extended, then bring the left foot over the right knee and place it flat on the floor, close to the right knee. Put your right hand on the left foot. Raise your left hand and bring it around your back with the palm open, hooking it around your waistline and stretching it as far back as you can. Inhale a deep breath and, while exhaling, slowly twist your head, shoulders and waist to the left, until you can twist no further. Keep the chin up and the shoulders level.

Remain in this position for a few seconds, holding your breath. Then inhale while slowly returning to the original position, without doing any brisk movements.

Repeat once more. Then change the position of the feet and hands and do the twist to the right side. Lie down and rest until your breathing becomes normal again. This is the first stage of the *Ardha-Matsyendrasana*.

Duration: Maintain this posture for several seconds, holding your breath. Gradually increase

Fig.3 *Ardha-Matsyendrasana*
The Twist Posture

the time to one minute. When holding it for more than a few seconds, resume the deep breathing while remaining in the posture. Repeat the twist two or three times.

Benefits: The *Ardha-Matsyendrasana* affects the adrenal glands. It also tones up sluggish kidneys and a congested liver and spleen. Asthma, constipation and indigestion, as well as obesity, are counteracted by the practice of this asana. The spine and its deep muscles are strengthened and rendered flexible; stooping shoulders, a bent back and defective posture are corrected. Asthma sufferers, especially, should emphasise the practice of this posture, along with the Shoulderstand, Reverse Posture and the Headstand or Half-headstand.

Second Stage: Start the second stage of the Twist Posture the following way: kneel down, then sit to the right side so that your feet are on your left side. Now place your left foot over your right knee, keeping the sole firmly on the mat. Next, put

Fig. 4 *Ardha-Matsyendrasana* — The Twist, Second Stage

your right hand on the left foot. Then raise your left hand and bring it to the back with the palm open, hooking it around the waistline as far as you can stretch it. Inhale a deep breath and, while exhaling, slowly twist to the utmost your head, shoulders and waist to the left, keeping the chin up.

Retain the posture for a while, holding your breath. Then slowly return to the original position, while inhaling, or inhale after returning to the original position. Repeat once more. Then change the position of your feet and hands by first kneeling, then sitting down to your left and keeping your right arm on the back with the palm open. Do the twisting movement to the right this time.

Final Stage: If you have been able to do this successfully, now try the last stage. First assume the position of the second stage sitting down to your right, with the left foot over the right knee and the left arm on the back with the open palm hooked around your waistline. Now, in the final movement, you keep your right hand on the left foot but you first slip your arm and elbow over to the other side of the left knee. Inhale a deep breath and exhale twisting to the left. Continue with the second stage until you find it possible to assume the complete posture. Pause for a while and

Fig. 5 *Ardha-Matsyendrasana*
The Twist, Final Stage

repeat the *Ardha-Matsyendrasana*. Then reverse the position of the legs and hands, and assume the same *asana* twisting to the right.

Variation of Final Stage: Instead of slipping your right arm over the left knee, you slip it under the knee and get hold of the left hand on the back.

Then inhale a deep breath and while exhaling twist to the left. Reverse the position of the legs and arms and do the twist to the right.

Ardha-Matsyendrasana, Sai Yoga Way

We shall now do the Sai Yoga Twist Posture. Kneel down and then sit to your right side with the legs and feet. Inhale a deep breath and assume the twist, turning your head, shoulders and waist to the left.

Close your eyes and imagine now that you are looking back at your past, whether it be yesterday or years ago. Examine some of the things in your life which you have done or which you have left undone.

Ponder over your actions, words or even thoughts for which you now feel regret... because thoughts have strength and can influence things, cause them to happen.

Think of something you yourself recognise as being a dark spot in your existence, something you feel sorry to have done... You would like now to correct this mistake, to erase this dark spot. So decide right now what you will do to make good, to rectify the error... You know you will not repeat it again. You are not any more a part of it, once you have recognised the wrong. You will try your best to make a change in the situation...

If the persons you have harmed are no longer on this earth, ask them to forgive you: they will hear you. If they are still alive, send them thoughts of love and Light, and also do whatever you can to undo the trouble and harm you have caused. Then cover it with Light and let it stay in the past, don't constantly bring it into the present. Don't let it 'eat you up' all the time.

Now, slowly unwind the twist and, after returning to the starting position, silently add some of your own words to what was said just now.

Then sit down to your left, or merely change the position of your legs and arms. Inhale a deep breath and slowly turn to your right while exhaling. Close your eyes, trying to imagine what your future life will be. You would like it to be a harmonious and happy one... You would like it to be straight, clean and shining... You then see a beam of bright light coming towards you from the distance. It forms a path which widens as it approaches you... Is this your life-path? Yes, it could be, if you really want to walk on it...

And now you become a little fearful...

Will I not soil it with my steps? Will I be able to stay on it without falling down? How will I reach the end when the path becomes more and more narrow?

As you are hesitating you hear a voice telling you:

"Don't be afraid. Come to me... Only, you must make the first steps and then I shall make the rest... I will always stay at your side... protect you and guide you...

"I will help you to walk straight and steady...

"I will hold your hand and lead you along the path...

"I am the Light...

"Come to me..." "Come..."

Om.

The Pelvic Posture - Vajrasana

Traditional Vajrasana

To assume the Pelvic Posture, you first kneel down, keep both your knees together and both feet apart. Now, sit down with your buttocks touching the floor between your legs. Place your palms on your thighs.

Duration: Retain the Pelvic Posture for as long as you comfortably can, doing the deep breathing.

Benefits: The *Vajrasana* helps relieve indigestion, gas and sciatica. It limbers all the joints of the legs and strengthens the muscles.

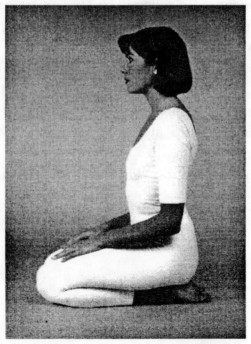

Fig. 6   *Vajrasana* — The Pelvic Posture

If you are not yet able to assume this posture, then sit down on your heels. You can put a pillow under your feet if they hurt. To be able eventually to assume the *Vajrasana* do the following: keeping your knees together and feet apart, do an up and down bouncing movement in an attempt to sit on the floor. If it helps, place your palms on the floor for support.

Vajrasana, Sai Yoga Way

Kneel down, keeping knees together and feet apart, so that you can sit between them. Put your palms on your thighs as you did earlier.

Now close your eyes and plan the rest of your day. Think of someone into whose life you could bring a bit of sunshine. Then ask yourself "Who am I?" And each time you breathe in, silently pronounce '*So*' followed by '*Ham*' on each exhalation. Your very breath constitutes a mantra: "*So*" meaning 'That' and '*Ham*' meaning 'I'. In this way, during every breath you answer the question "Who am I?," by constantly repeating "I am That, I am That, I am That." Another common Sanskrit expression referring to the same subject is: "*Tat twam asi*" (You are that).

If you drop the '*S*' in '*So*' and the '*Ha*' in '*Ham*,' you are left with *Om*.

Do this each day starting with half a minute and gradually increase the time.

The Supine Pelvic Posture
Supta Vajrasana

Traditional Supta Vajrasana

Do not attempt to assume the Supine Pelvic Posture until you are very comfortable in the Pelvic Posture. First sit down in the *Vajrasana*, then, placing your elbows on the floor behind your back, slowly glide down until your entire back rests on the floor. Place your palms under your neck. Do not curve your spine: it should be as straight as possible. Close your eyes and breathe deeply.

Duration: Maintain the *Supta Vajrasana* for as long as you comfortably can, then slowly return to the sitting position. Stretch out both legs and lie down to rest.

Benefits: This posture invigorates and strengthens the pelvic organs, the viscera, abdomen and the nerves which are connected with sex functions.

Caution: If you cannot assume this posture easily do not force yourself into it. Instead, just lie down flat on the floor with your palms under your neck.

Supta Vajrasana, Sai Yoga Way

Having assumed the *Supta Vajrasana* close your eyes and slowly do the deep breathing. Imagine now that you are a butterfly resting on a lotus leaf... with wings spread out to relax. It seems that everything around you is humming with a rhythmic sound. As you listen to it you begin to wonder whether this enchanting melody flows from the birds, the insects, the rustling treetops or from your heart. It seems that this song is in everything and you begin to feel such a closeness to nature around you...

Fig. 7 *Supta Vajrasana* — The Supine Pelvic Posture

It is very beautiful, but you would not like to stay here always. You do not want to be attached to the ground, not even to a green leaf or a flower petal. You want to be free... to fly towards the sun, into limitless space... among the myriad stars... and from there to look down on the earth.

It was so pleasant to take a rest there for a while, but not to remain there forever, since you would then become a part of the wingless world which is unable to fly. And so it is with your soul, with your heart. They can always fly to the blue heights and come close to the goal... to your real home, which is the Kingdom of Light.

To be a messenger of Light is a great joy, to bring it into the lives of those who have forgotten the real meaning of love, truth, righteousness and peace.

Now stretch out to take a rest. As you are lying on the floor, imagine that you are feeling the pulsation of the earth below you and the dancing of the sun's rays above you. Everything is light and sound and you merge into the All by chanting *Om*.

The Reverse Posture - Viparita Karani Mudra

Traditional Viparita Karani Mudra

Lie down on your back. Then take a deep breath and raise your legs and the lower part of your body off the floor. Quickly put your hands on your back to support it, keeping the thumbs under the hip bones. The elbows on the floor should be kept close to each other, otherwise they will not give adequate support to the body, and you will find it difficult to stay in the Reverse Posture. Hold the legs straight up with toes pointed. Do not bend the knees.

Remain in this position with your eyes closed, doing deep breathing. You may feel some discomfort in the beginning, especially in the elbows, but this will pass.

Duration: In the beginning you will be able to keep this posture for only a few seconds, but gradually, with practice, you can increase its duration to about ten minutes.

Benefits: This *Viparita Karani Mudra* affects primarily the sex gland and the thyroid glands. It helps to keep the glands, organs and skin in a youthful condition, preventing premature aging of the body. Practise this *mudra* in order to remain youthful. It is very beneficial for female disorders, painful or irregular menstruation, and mental or physical stress during menopause. It also restores and preserves vigour in men.

Preparatory Exercise

If you have trouble assuming this posture then try the following exercise first. Sit down on the floor in front of a table, with your legs stretched under it. Make sure you are close enough to the table so that your forehead can touch the edge without leaning forward. Then lie down and bring your feet up against the edge of the table, pressing it with the middle of the soles, not the heels or toes. Raise your body off the floor and support it with both hands under the hip bones. Keep the elbows close together on the floor. Remain in this posture for a while doing the Deep Breathing.

After a few days you can try to straighten your legs one by one, keeping them in an upright position, or slightly inclined towards the floor behind the head.

Viparita Karani Mudra, Sai Yoga Way

Assume the *Viparita Karani Mudra*. Close your eyes. In this position, your feet, which are always touching the darkness of the ground, are now close to the sky. They are the first to receive the rays of Light which stream down from the tip of your toes, filling your entire being. And this is because you have changed the position of your body, reversing it.

Fig.8 *Viparita Karani Mudra*
The Reverse Posture

You can also do likewise by reversing a situation in your life. No matter how hopeless it may seem at first, you can find a way out of it. Whenever you feel depressed, defeated, lonely or unhappy, you only have to remember that you have a friend who is always by your side to guide you out of the darkness of despair. You know that when you are unable to lift yourself up or to reach out towards the Light, the Giver of Light will always help you. There is always a way out of the darkness... no matter how dense and hopeless it may seem. When a door is closed, look for the window. You cannot imagine how often things can become right when you try the Reverse, asking for guidance believing you have someone, a friend, who will never let you down. That friend is forever: He is the Light; He is God; He is Truth; He is Love. *Om*.

The Shoulderstand - Sarvangasana

Traditional Sarvangasana

You can get into the *Sarvangasana* from the Reverse Posture by moving your palms lower down towards the shoulders (closer to the ground) and completely straightening your back. Support it with both hands, keeping the elbows as close together as possible and let the body rest on the shoulders and the nape of the neck. Keep your body as straight as a candle. Press the chin against the chest, straighten the knees and point the toes. Close your eyes and breathe deeply, trying to remain steady in this position.

Maintain the *Sarvangasana* as long as you comfortably can. Then, on an exhalation, return slowly to the ground, gradually lowering the back. Unroll it so that it touches the floor vertebra by vertebra. When you reach a position of 90 degrees from the hips, stop for a second, straighten the knees, take a deep breath and slowly lower your legs to the ground while breathing out.

Duration: Retain this posture for about fifteen seconds, gradually working up to six minutes. If the Shoulderstand is done alone, without any other postures to precede or follow, it can be retained from fifteen to twenty minutes by an advanced student.

Benefits: *Sarvangasana* affects, primarily, the thyroid gland and also the sex glands. It has an influence upon the metabolism, tones the nerves and acts as a blood purifier, especially helping cases of poor blood circulation. Its practice also strengthens the lower organs, helping to keep them in place. This *asana* is especially recommended for women after childbirth. People troubled by asthma, constipation, indigestion, disorders of the kidneys, bladder, ureter and urethra should diligently practise this posture. It is also helpful in overcoming seminal weakness in men and painful menstruation as well as other disorders in women.

Fig.9 *Sarvangasana*
The Shoulderstand

Caution: The Shoulderstand should not be practised by a person with organic disorders of the thyroid gland, and should be done cautiously by anyone suffering from chronic nasal catarrh.

Sarvangasana, Sai Yoga Way

In the Shoulderstand, you rise higher to be still closer to the sky. Close your eyes and imagine that you are a candle, a white candle, in the Temple of Light... burning for the glory of the Giver of Lights.

And you know that by standing tall and keeping the flame steady you are going to help those who will be attracted by the lights in the Temple... people who have lost their faith... who are falling under the burden of their difficulties... or of their bad habits... And seeing these candles, straight and unflickering, they slowly start believing that there is Light, that there is Truth, that there is God.

You inspire them by being a straight candle in the Temple of Light... you will never melt into a crooked misshapen candle... you will always remain standing tall and beautiful, an ever-glowing light that will not be blown out even in the stormy darkness.

As a human being you are a messenger of Light on this earth... you are the only creature that has a straight vertical spine... all the others have a horizontal one. So, you are meant to be a connecting link between earth and heaven. Remain this way throughout your life. Don't succumb... don't bend... don't extinguish your flame... remain forever a shining candle in the Temple of Light. *Om.*

The Plough Posture - Halasana

Traditional Halasana

It is easier to do the Plough Posture, the *Halasana*, if you first get into the Reverse Posture or the Shoulderstand. Inhale deeply, then slowly, without bending the knees, if possible, start lowering both legs while exhaling. When the toes touch the ground behind your head, you have assumed the Plough Posture.

Put your palms on the floor or let them support the back. Retain this posture for a while doing the deep breathing. This might be a little uncomfortable at first, but soon it will become easier for you. Next, return to the lying position while exhaling. Slowly uncurve the spine, vertebra by vertebra, until it touches the floor. You accomplish this by slightly bending your knees, then slowly gliding them down over your face, almost touching it. Continue this slow motion unfolding of the entire posture.

Duration: Retain this posture for five seconds to start with, add a few seconds each week until you can hold it for about five minutes. Repeat from two to four times, increasing the number only after fourteen days.

Benefits: The Plough Posture has a stimulating effect on the thyroid gland, it also massages the liver and spleen; it stretches and pulls the vertebrae thereby maintaining youthfulness, flexibility and a healthy spine. This posture is especially beneficial for people who suffer from obesity, enlarged liver and spleen, constipation, indigestion, stiffness, muscular rheumatism and arthritis.

Caution: Do not attempt to touch the floor with your toes unless you have a naturally flexible spine. It is helpful to do the following preliminary exercise: lie down with the head about two feet away from the wall – if you are tall the distance will have to be proportionately farther – and assume the Reverse Posture. Now, lower your legs until your toes reach the wall and, keeping the knees straight, start 'walking down' the wall. Make sure you don't force the walking any lower than is comfortable for your spine, since you might injure a rigid muscle. The resulting pain may last for several weeks and you should shy away from trying the Plough again.

Variation

While in the *Halasana*, you may do the following exercise: inhale a deep breath and, keeping the toes and heels together, make a semicircular movement with them to the right, while exhaling. Return to the centre and repeat the same to the left.

Now, inhale deeply and, while exhaling, make a semicircular movement with both feet, gliding the right foot to the right and the left foot to the left. Keep the legs apart this way for a little while, then join the feet together again and return to the prone position. Finally, slowly and gradually release the Plough Posture as already instructed.

Fig. 10   *Halasana* — The Plough Posture

Halasana, Sai Yoga Way

Assume the *Halasana*. Then close your eyes and imagine that the tips of your toes are charged with Light which will dispel the darkness of the earth that surrounds you, the darkness of the material world... Then you make a protective circle of Light around you. Keep your feet together and move them first to the right and then to the left side... Visualize the circle of Light protecting you so that no evil can touch you and no dark force can harm you... You are now guarded by the Light from the gloomy and cheerless world of depression and darkness.

You can always protect yourself if you call for help on the Divine forces from above... You don't have to succumb to that which is low and base... or that which comes from the kingdom of darkness. Always remember you belong to the Kingdom of Light... Nothing can prevent you from rising higher and higher above the unhappy situations in life. You will replace these sunless spots with the brightly glowing Light of Love... One step upwards can always be followed by many more. The Light in your heart will protect you from everything that can hold you back, can pull you down, and prevent you from rising.

Stay in this position and think of something that happened in your life, something you realise has been pulling you down... And if you only keep on believing in the Light, even if you have made a step down, it is not for long... You will be able to take a leap up again because the light forces will always protect you when you ask for help. *Om*.

The Lotus Pose - Padmasana

Traditional Padmasana

Padmasana is the classical meditative posture. Sit on the mat with both legs extended. Then bend the right knee, get hold of the right foot with both hands and place it on your left thigh as high as possible, so that the heel touches the abdomen. Then do the same with your left leg crossing it over the right leg and placing your left foot on your right thigh as high as possible. Both heels should be close together. Now, put your hands on your knees, close your eyes and do deep breathing, keeping the spine absolutely straight.

Duration: Remain in the *Padmasana* for as long as you can comfortably keep this posture, gradually increasing the time of retention.

Benefits: The Lotus Posture alone has no special therapeutic value, except having a calming effect on the mind and helping concentration.

Preliminary Exercise

If you cannot assume the Lotus Pose, do the following exercise. First extend both legs and place your right sole against the left thigh, or on the thigh if that is easier for you. Now, begin bouncing the right knee up and down; this movement should not be forced but rather done as gentle flapping. Repeat the same with the left leg.

Next, keep the soles of your feet together and continue the flapping movement using both knees to resemble the movement of a flying bird. For most people, especially Occidentals, this exercise is indispensable for getting into the

Lotus Pose. I did it for six months before I was able to assume the *Padmasana!*

Padmasana, Sai Yoga Way
Concentration And Meditation

Someone has said, "The power of concentration makes the difference between a genius and an ordinary man."

Concentration can be positive or negative, selfless or selfish, all depending on the way it is directed. If one concentrates upon fulfilling a certain desire, it is best to add something like: "If this is right for me", or, in other words, "Thy will be done". In most cases when we say this, we want things to happen the way we would like them to. But this would be superimposing our will over the Divine Will. And this one should never do unless you are prepared to pay for it sooner or later. As

Fig. 11 *Padmasana* — The Lotus Pose

J. Krishnamurti once said in his discourse, "Be careful of what you wish: you may get it."

To cultivate the power of concentration, I would suggest the following exercise. Sit down comfortably in front of a lighted candle so that the flame is more or less at eye level and between two to five feet away. Take a deep breath and fix your gaze steadily on the light of the candle. Don't tense up, however, since this may lead into a state of self-hypnosis and produce a headache or some other discomfort.

After a while, you will feel that the vision of the flame is fixed in your mind; close your eyes, retaining this vision so that you continue to see the flame with closed eyes. If you don't, or it escapes you, open your eyes again and continue looking at the flame. Then close them and try once more. You can repeat this several times until you succeed in seeing the light with your mind's eye. It may happen that you will see the flame in a different colour, or it may seem to be moving away from you, receding further and further. Sometimes you may even see the light as being dark and the background bright. As long as you keep your mind steadied on the flame, it doesn't matter.

Continue practising this exercise for a few minutes each day and your power of concentration will gradually increase and give you the possibility of achieving things with minimum effort, especially in the creative, artistic or business fields, but, above all, in meditation.

Concentration is a great aid for successful meditation. But most Occidentals are not in the habit of practising it and find it difficult to keep their minds on any one object for a length of time. Usually their thoughts jump from one object to another, like monkeys in a jungle. A large number of people also do not understand the difference between concentration and meditation. Concentration is keeping the mind fixed on one object to the exclusion of all else. Meditation is merging with the chosen image.

If you are meditating on the Light, the first stage would be: "I am walking in the Light." The second stage would make you feel "The Light is in me." And lastly "I am the Light." Then you, the meditator, and the act of meditation disappear, and only the Light, or the object, remains. Meditation is a spiritual process, and has nothing to do with any material gains and desires.

To start with, one meditates upon a form until one is able to go over to the formless. The object must be of a spiritual nature, elevating, uplifting, beautiful. Meditation is transcendental: you are not aware of yourself, the time or your surroundings. Only someone far advanced is able to leave meditating on the form and go over to the formless: spiritual giants are able to achieve this. For myself, I am perfectly satisfied to meditate on the form.

In the beginning, it is essential to adhere to a fixed time and place, to sit with a perfectly straight back in any meditative posture in which you feel comfortable. The *Padmasana* is perfect for this. Before starting on meditation, you may do the *Omkar*, repeat your mantra if you have one, or sing some devotional songs. Now light the incense and candle and assume the Lotus Posture. Close your eyes and imagine that inside your heart a flower is slowly opening its petals and in the centre you perceive a quite brilliant light... It has always been there and always will. Only, in some instances, it may have been covered by many layers which prevented that Light from shining forth. Layers of anger, envy, hatred, jealously, selfishness, greed, vulgarity, pettiness and so on.

Now let this Light fill your entire being. Bring it also to your lips so that no ugly words or curses should pass through them. Then bring the Light to your eyes, so that they should not see base or vulgar things, even if looking at them. Do the same to your ears, so that no sounds coming from the world of darkness should affect you. Then bring that Light to your forehead, to cleanse your mind and thoughts. Finally, take it still higher, up above your head where it shines like a crown of little lights that attract the rays of the Great Eternal Light... They fall over you like a golden rain, which forms a protective veil around you, so that no forces of darkness should be able to harm you.

And now imagine that you are at the bottom of some white, marble-like steps which go up so high that you cannot see where they end. But you know that they lead to the Kingdom of Light Eternal, to the Abode of the One who gave is the source of Light... and carrying the Light in your heart, you begin to walk up... With every step forward, the Light within you gets a little brighter... As you go up and up, the steps get higher and narrower, and the goal is still far away... But you do not give up. Finally you reach a wide platform, where you sit down before continuing your journey, and meditate upon the Eternal Divine Light and the form it took to save you and me. *Om.*

The Fish Posture - Matsyasana

Traditional Matsyasana

The classical way to do the *Matsyasana* is to first assume the Lotus Posture. Then recline backwards, propping yourself up on the elbows and arching the spine. Throw your head back and glide the elbows forward until the crown of your head touches the ground. The back and shoulders should be kept off the mat by the arched spine. Take hold of your toes with your hands and begin to do the deep breathing.

If you are not yet able to assume the Lotus Posture, just sit with crossed legs, tailor fashion, before bending back. Then recline backwards, propping yourself up on the elbows and arching the spine. Throw your head back and glide the elbows forward until the crown of your head touches the ground. By your arched spine, your back and shoulders should be kept well off the mat. Grasp your toes with your hands and begin doing deep breathing.

Duration: Remain in this position for as long as you comfortably can.

Benefits: The Fish Posture strengthens the back and invigorates the nervous system. It beautifies, limbers and strengthens the neck. Asthma and bronchitis are greatly relieved by the practice of the *Matsyasana*. This posture regulates the proper functioning of the pituitary, pineal, thyroid and adrenal glands. It is said that in this posture you can float on the surface of the water. I must confess that I haven't as yet tried to do so!

Matsyasana, Sai Yoga Way

Assume the *Matsyasana* the best way you can. Then close your eyes and slowly, doing deep rhythmic breathing, imagine yourself floating on an ocean with the endless blue sky above you. It feels so good to be carried by the gentle waves... to be so relaxed and almost weightless, like a flower petal tossed into the water... The setting sun turns the water around you golden and it seems that you are now floating on an ocean of light... careless and free... without the fear of sinking... And it begins to dawn on you that in the same way you can also float above the vicissitudes of life... that you don't have to succumb and to go under... Keep the name of the Giver of Light in your heart, and your faith strong and unshakable, and you will never sink to the bottom.

With the help of your mind, which should be strong and healthy, you should be able to cross the ocean of life...

Give up all your fears and doubts... surrender to the Higher Will. If you say in your heart "Thy will be done" and really mean it, you don't have to worry about anything.

Let the Supreme Being guide your destiny and steer you through the stormy ocean of life...

You are His child...

A child of Light... Now and forever... *Om*.

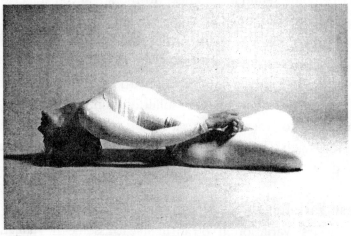

Fig. 12 *Matsyasana* — The Fish Posture

Yoga Mudra - The Symbol of Yoga

Traditional Yoga Mudra

The classical way of doing the *Yoga Mudra* is, first, to assume the Lotus Pose of *Padmasana*. Then, keeping both hands behind the back, your left wrist clasped by the right hand, inhale a deep breath and, while exhaling, slowly bend forward until your forehead (and chin) reaches the floor. Do not raise your arms, let them rest on your back.

Remain in this position, holding your breath. Then slowly sit up. If you stay in the *Yoga Mudra* for a prolonged time, don't hold your breath. Just continue doing Deep Breathing.

Duration: Keep the posture for as long as you comfortably can. Soon you will be able to retain it for several minutes.

Benefits: In its initial stage, *Yoga Mudra* increases the peristaltic movement of the bowels and helps against constipation. It also strengthens the abdominal muscles, tones the nervous system and massages the pelvic region. It helps men to overcome seminal weakness. In the advanced stage, when *Yoga Mudra* is retained for a great length of time (from half an hour to 3 hours) it induces the awakening of the dormant *Kundalini* (creative energy coiled up at the end of the spinal column), but only in conjunction with other Yoga practices.

Caution: For a person suffering from constipation, it is important to practice the *Yoga Mudra* very gently. Release the posture each time slowly, without rapid or jerking movements. Lie down and rest before proceeding to another posture.

Easy Variations

First Variation: If you are unable to assume the *Padmasana*, begin by sitting up straight and keeping both legs crossed tailor

Fig. 13 *Yoga Mudra*
The Symbol of Yoga

fashion. Clench both fists and keep them a little below the navel on both sides of the abdomen.

Take a deep breath and, while exhaling, bend forward as far as possible, still pressing the fists into the abdomen. Remember, they must be pressed, not just held there. Stay in this position for a few seconds and then return to the erect position again.

Second Variation: If you have difficulty sitting cross-legged, then begin by kneeling on the floor and press your clenched fists into the sides of your abdomen while bending forward.

Third Variation: A still easier way to do the *Yoga Mudra* is by sitting on the edge of a hard chair keeping the knees and feet wide apart. Then inhale a deep breath and, while exhaling, bend forward lowering your head as far as you can.

Fig. 14 *Yoga Mudra* — The Symbol of Yoga

Yoga Mudra, Sai Yoga Way

Assume any of the variations of the *Yoga Mudra* you are comfortable in and close your eyes. Now think of your body as being a temple of the Living Spirit, and your heart as the altar on which the Light is burning... And you are the High Priest (or High Priestess) of this temple... It was given into your custody and it is your sacred duty to take good care of it... to maintain it clean and beautiful, free of all dust... the dust of anger, hatred, greed, envy, jealousy, lust, malice, pride, haughtiness and the like. And to keep the Light on the altar burning brightly at all times, not just flickering... you must keep fanning the flame with good deeds, kind words and pure thoughts... keeping away from everything ugly, base and vulgar... making the Light grow bigger and clearer day by day so that every corner of the temple should be brightly lit... driving away all darkness... since light and darkness do not live together.

Try now to fill your heart with Light... Love, compassion, friendliness... and after doing that offer it to the Giver of Light... to the Creator of all things and beings. To your *Ishtadeva*, your chosen deity.

Now inhale a deep breath and slowly bow down to offer the Light of your heart to the one who is the source of all Light and all life. This offering is greater than any flowers, incense, candles, or anything else; the pure Light of your heart... the greatest gift you possess... It is the only real treasure you have; everything else is here today and gone tomorrow... There is nothing else you can call your own: your family, friends, your positions, possessions, even health and strength, all these you may lose any moment. And you yourself will leave all these behind when you depart for good from your body. You can take nothing with you, except the Light of your heart and the thoughts and deeds dictated by it... Offering it does not mean that the Light of your heart will diminish or become extinct. On the contrary, by merging with the eternal Divine Light it will become one with it, the way a drop of water, when tossed into the ocean, becomes a part of the ocean.

Remaining in the *Yoga Mudra*, continue forming your own words to express your devotion, love, gratitude and surrender to the Supreme, experiencing the closeness to that which is Light, which is Love, which is God. *Om.*

The Headstand - Shirshasana

Traditional Shirshasana

Having taught *yoga asanas* for over thirty-five years, I have found that the way described below is the safest, surest and easiest way to learn the Headstand. Just follow the instructions carefully.

The Half-Headstand:

We will begin with this. Place a pad, which is not too thick, on the floor. Kneel down and interlock your fingers, slightly cupping the palms, and place them on the pad, keeping elbows close to each other. Now, put the top of your head on the pad nesting it in your cupped hands. Straighten the knees, raise them off the floor and take a few small steps towards the head, walking on the tips of your toes. Stay in this position for a few seconds, doing Deep Breathing. Then, lower your knees to a kneeling position, straighten your body and raise both arms while inhaling deeply. Lie down and rest until your breathing returns to normal. This is imperative. Continue doing this for a week or longer, for just a few minutes a day. Remember that if the Headstand is contraindicate do not attempt the Half-headstand either.

Practising headstand:

First Stage: Let us now try to do the Headstand in the corner. Have someone helping you. Place a pad in the corner and place your cupped hands with the fingers interlocked, in the very corner. Now proceed as you did in the Half-headstand: put your head down and with your knees bent take a few steps towards your head. Now raise your right leg as high as you can and let the person assisting you grasp by the ankle (if your assistant stands on the left side, you should raise the left leg and count aloud "one-two-three" and say "hop" to give a signal). You then make a little jump with the other leg while your assistant places your right leg into the corner between the walls. Your left leg will follow of its own accord. Your assistant should steady you by keeping both hands on your ankles or by stretching an arm across the corner to prevent you from losing your balance and falling. Relax the neck and don't arch the back.

Remain in this position for fifteen seconds, then come down slow, one foot at a time, with the toes inverted or you may hurt them badly. It might help to have the person helping you hold the ankle of one foot while you lower the other. After standing up, raise your arms while taking a deep breath; then lie down and relax until your breath returns to normal.

Fig. 15 *Shirshasana* — The Headstand

Second Stage: After practising the *Shirshasana* in the corner for at least a week or so, you may now try to do it against a wall.

First kneel down and measure the distance by placing your right wrist against the wall and marking the spot out where your elbow is. Place the pad in this position and place your cupped hands there, with fingers interlocked, to nestle your head in. Do not place the top of your head on your fingers: it should rest on the mat. Keep your elbows as close together as possible, since the weight of your body should be placed on your forearms as well as on the head. Now get up from your knees, take a few little steps forward, making a jumping movement so as to get your feet off the ground and up against the wall. Now you have the soles of your feet on the wall for support. Keep the knees bent so that your back remains absolutely straight. Don't arch it.

Keep practising the Headstand in this position without attempting to straighten the knees for the first few days. It is better to do it after several days of practice with the support of the wall first, to give you confidence and a better sense of balance. Never lean against the wall with the legs stretched out as this will throw the entire body into a strained incorrect position. Tuck in the buttocks and remember not to arch the spine while in this position. This is a common mistake with self-taught people.

Stay in this position for about thirty seconds, then come down slowly one leg at a time, or with both feet, keeping the knees bent. Inhale a deep breath with arms outstretched and lie down to rest.

When your are able to do the Headstand easily with the support of the wall, you may try to straighten your knees and remain like this for a few seconds, without straining and stiffening the body. As soon as you begin to lose your balance, quickly bend your knees again and prop your feet against the wall. Slowly lower your feet to the floor remembering to land on inverted toes. Stand up straight, take a deep breath with arms upraised and lie down to relax.

Third Stage: When you are able to remain steady on your head without the support of the wall, you may finally try the *Shirshasana* in the middle of the room. Put the pad on the floor and place a big pillow behind it, since your first attempt may end up in a somersault! Get into the Half-headstand, take a deep breath and, with a gentle kick, get both legs off the floor and start raising them as you did when you had the wall to support you, still keeping the knees bent. Next, tuck in the buttocks before straightening your legs, otherwise you will

Fig.16 *Shirshasana* — The Headstand

definitely lose your balance. Keep your body erect without arching the back, toes pointed, elbows not too far apart so that the weight of your body is properly distributed between the forearms and head. Relax the muscles of your neck and close your eyes.

Do deep breathing while holding the posture, then slowly come down. Inhale deeply while raising the arms, and lie down to relax.

Duration: Hold the Headstand for fifteen to twenty seconds initially, gradually increasing the time by about fifteen seconds per week. Ten to twelve minutes is the maximum for the Headstand if it is done along with the other postures.

Benefits: The *Shirshasana* affects the pituitary and pineal glands situated inside the skull. They, in turn, regulate the proper functioning of the thyroid, parathyroid, adrenal and sex glands, which influence the well-being of the whole organism. In the Headstand the pull of gravity is diminished hence it has a relaxing effect – after you learn to do it with ease, of course. It is highly beneficial for people suffering from tension, fatigue, headaches, constipation, asthma, sleeplessness, nervousness, poor blood circulation, bad memory, congested throat, and the early stages of eye and nose trouble. It is recommended for people with a sluggish liver or spleen. The Headstand also counteracts lack of energy and vitality, and helps to get self-confidence enhancing the joy of living. It is excellent for women suffering from female disorders and for improving muscle tone after childbirth.

Caution: The Headstand is not to be done if one's blood pressure is below 100 or above 150, or after a recent operation or injury. It should also be avoided by those suffering from running or pussing ears, chronic nasal catarrh, nose bleeding[1], and weak eye capillaries, when the whites of the eyes easily get bloodshot. Women should not do it during their monthly periods, and persons whose pituitary, pineal and thyroid glands have some organic defects also should not do it. The same applies to those who being constipated are passing an excessively dry stool. If standing on the head produces palpitations or dizziness one should wait until these conditions disappear.

The *Shirshasana* should always be done on an empty stomach, at the beginning rather that at the end of your exercise period, before you begin to get tired. However, it is also good to do when you are hungry, nervous, unhappy and when you need a tonic to 'pep you up'. Do it when you want to feel relaxed, when the brain is clouded and when you are in low spirits. Do it when your thoughts are distracted and you cannot concentrate properly. It is much easier to meditate and relax after doing the Headstand, which is very aptly called the King of *asanas*.

Fig. 17 *Shirshasana* — The Headstand

Shirshasana, Sai Yoga Way

Get into the Headstand or else the Half-headstand. Close your eyes and imagine yourself as a tree... your head representing the roots, which are the most important part of it... and your body the trunk, growing straight up towards the skies. You are a tree with many branches that are covered not only by leaves but also by beautiful white flowers... But they are different from any other flowers because each one of them has a Light in its heart... flowers of light. You are standing on a hill so that everyone can see you, even from a distance... a miracle tree... At night you look like a bright Christmas tree... and people come from near and far to look at you in amazement... They marvel at these wounderous flowers like small children... And their hearts begin to open up to the Light... You have given them a ray of hope. They stretch out their hands, and you drop a little flower into each outstretched palm, so they may take it home with them and continue believing in miracles. Miracles of the Light, miracles of God. And the more you give, the more flowers appear on your branches. You experience the joy of giving without asking anything in return. You can bring Light into the life of everyone who needs a little more love... a little more compassion... understanding... and friendliness. Untouched and unmoved by those who may disbelieve and laugh at you, you go on spreading the gospel of Light. You have everything, the Light lives in every flower of your thoughts and deeds. So let it always sing in your heart, shine in your heart, dance in your heart, until you see nothing but this Light... and become one with it... Forever... *Om*.

The Sun Salutation - Surya Namaskar

Surya Namaskar is a Sanskrit term meaning, literally, 'Sun Greeting'. Yoga students in India usually perform this exercise at sunrise, fixing their eyes upon the rising sun. If performed indoors, the *surya* (sun) is imagined or a worthy image is chosen instead.

Affecting and revitalising most of the vital parts and organs of our body this is really a series of nine exercises grouped together, and serves as a complete routine for the student. The late Raja (King) of Aundh, a great advocate of the *Surya Namaskar* and the man who introduced it into the schools of this State, says it is an "exercise for health, efficiency and longevity"[2].

Preliminary Exercise for Surya Namaskar

Assume the 'board position' of the *Surya Namaskar*. Inhale a deep breath and while holding it, bend the elbows to lower the body, then straighten them again. It is like doing push ups. Do this several times, then exhale to lower the body to the ground. If it is difficult for you as a beginner to slowly lower your body, practise this exercise several times, because it is a necessary part of the *Surya Namaskar*.

The *Surya Namaskar* begins as follows:

1. Place a mat or a towel in front of you on the floor, stand with your toes touching the edge of it, keeping your spine and head erect and your feet together. Firmly press the palms – held at chest level – against each other (Fig. 18).

2. Inhale a deep breath and retain it while slowly raising the arms and bending your body backward (Fig. 19).

3. Now, bend forward while exhaling, letting your palms rest on the mat. Let your forehead touch your knees. Remember,

Fig. 18

Fig. 19

The Sun Salutation

Fig. 20

Fig. 21

Fig. 25

Fig. 24

Surya Namaskar

Fig. 23

Fig. 22

don't force yourself into any position, relax into it. From now on do not move the palms: they remain rooted to the mat throughout the entire exercise (Fig. 20).

4. Take another deep breath, hold it and stretch the right leg out backwards, bending the knee slightly (Fig. 21).

The left leg immediately follows the right one so that both feet are side by side, with toes inverted and knees touching the floor.

5. Next, quickly bring your knees off the floor and stiffen your entire body to resemble a straight board (Fig. 22).

Then start exhaling while slowly lowering your body to the floor by bending your elbows as if doing a push up (Fig. 23). Keep your buttocks as high as possible, so that your chin and chest meet the ground first. Then glide along the floor as the buttocks lower and the stomach makes contact with the floor. The movement is done fast.

6. Straighten the elbows, inhale a deep breath and throw the head back. This brings us to the position shown in (Fig. 24).

7. Exhaling, assume the position of an inverted V. All your weight should rest on your palms and the soles of your feet which should be flat on the floor. Keep your head in line with your back (Fig. 26).

8. Inhale and move the right foot forward so that your thigh presses firmly against your right side. Then quickly straighten the left leg and stand up. Exhale bending forward until the forehead touches the knees. This will bring you back to the position shown in (Fig. 21).

9. Lastly, raise your body up, while inhaling, throw your arms up and bend your body back (Fig. 20). Hold for a moment, then exhaling return to the original position, palms at chest level pressed firmly together (Fig. 19).

During the second round, you repeat the same movements but in reverse. First stretch out the left leg, and when, at the end, you return to the original position, move the left leg forward first. Continue to alternate legs with every round. The whole routine should be performed without pauses, the movements flowing from one to the other in quick succession. This makes it possible to do one round while taking four breaths. It may be done in three breaths if you omit the inhalation in the last movement. As you progress, you may finally end up doing the entire *Surya Namaskar* in one breath.

Having completed the *Surya Namaskar*, lie down and relax until your breathing returns to normal.

In India the *Surya Namaskars* are usually accompanied by the recitation of some *Vedic* mantras, known as the *Bija* mantras, intoning the various names of the Sun, the Prime Life-giving Source:

Om Hram Mitraya Namah - Om Hreem Ravaye Namah - Om Hroom Suryaya Namah - Om Hraim Bhanawe Namah - Om Hraum Khagaya Namah - Om Hrah Pushne Namah - Om Hram Hiranyagarbhaya Namah - Om Hreem Mareechaye Namah - Om Hroom Adityaya Namah - Om Hraim Savitre Namah - Om Hraum Arkaya Namah - Om Hrah Bhaskaraya Namah.

Benefits: The movements that constitute the *Surya Namaskar* will help make your body more agile and flexible even though you may not be doing them perfectly in the beginning. The *Surya Namaskar* affects the digestive, respiratory and nervous systems, and is highly recommended for people suffering from constipation, liver troubles, indigestion, colds, coughs, asthma, headaches, mental fatigue, depression, insomnia and nervousness. In addition to the benefits already mentioned, it endows those who practise it diligently with youth, better health, greater vitality, stronger muscles, a toned nervous system, a more efficient circulatory system and an overall feeling of well-being.

If you wish to quicken the results of the exercise, allow your mind to concentrate on the parts of your body you want affected, visualising the organ or region of the body. Follow each movement until you become the movement.

Duration: Providing that no other exercises are done, an adult who is doing the *Surya Namaskar* may do approximately twenty five rounds daily for a start. Then the number may be gradually increased. In the beginning, it is best to do the exercises no longer than ten minutes each day, preferable in the morning before breakfast, on an empty stomach.

Caution: Not to be done by persons suffering from very high or low blood pressure, or a weak heart; also when contraindicated by a physician especially after an operation or prolonged illness.

End Notes:

1. Eating a raw onion a day may help against nose bleeding and weak eye capillaries.
2. Author of The Ten Point Way to Health, London, J. M. Dent & Sons.

OUR PUBLICATIONS

01. 70 QS & AS. ON PRACTICAL SPIRITUALITY AND SATHYA SAI BABA	- O. P. Vidyakar	Rs. 90
02. A COMPENDIUM OF THE TEACHINGS OF SATHYA SAI BABA(4th Ed.)	- Charlene Leslie-Chadan	Rs. 600
03. "ALEX" THE DOLPHIN	- Lightstrom	Rs. 90
04. A JOURNEY TO LOVE (4th Ed.)	- David Bailey	Rs. 180
05. A JOURNEY TO LOVE BOOK II Love & Marriage	- David Bailey	Rs. 200
06. A JOURNEY TO LOVE (Spanish)	- David Bailey	Rs. 375
07. A JOURNEY TO LOVE (Telugu)	- David Bailey	Rs. 60
08. ANOTHER JOURNEY TO LOVE	- Faye Bailey	Rs. 200
09. ASHES, ASHES WE ALL FALL DOWN	- Gloria St. John	Rs. 80
10. A STORY OF INDIA AND PATAL BHUVANESWAR	- Jennifer Warren	Rs. 60
11. AT THE FEET OF SAI	- R. Lowenberg	Rs. 120
12. BAPU TO BABA	- V. K. Narasimhan	Rs. 120
13. BUDO-KA - True Spiritual Warriors	- Deena Naidu	Rs. 200
14. CRICKET FOR LOVE	- Sai Towers	Rs. 250
15. CUTTING THE TIES THAT BIND	- Phyllis Krystal	Rs. 110
16. CUTTING THE TIES THAT BIND Symbol Cards	- Phyllis Krystal	Rs. 120
17. CUTTING THE TIES THAT BIND - Posters	- Phyllis Krystal	Rs. 600
18. CUTTING MORE TIES THAT BIND	- Phyllis Krystal	Rs. 120
19. CUTTING THE TIES THAT BIND - Work Book	- Phyllis Krystal	Rs. 140
20. DA PUTTAPARTHIA PATAL BHUVANESHWAR (Italian)	- Sandra Percy	Rs. 150
21. DEATHING (Indian Edition)	- Anya Foos-Graber	Rs. 195
22. DISCOVERING MARTIAL ARTS	- Deena Naidu	Rs. 265
23. EDUCATION IN HUMAN VALUES (3 Vols.)	- June Auton	Rs. 750
24. FACE TO FACE WITH GOD	- V. I. K. Sarin	Rs. 150
25. GLIMPSES OF THE DIVINE	- Birgitte Rodriguez	Rs. 150
26. GLORY OF SAI PADHUKAS	- Sai Towers	Rs. 100
27. GOD AND HIS GOSPEL	- Dr. M. N.Rao	Rs. 120
28. GOD LIVES IN INDIA	- R. K. Karanjia	Rs. 75
29. GOD DESCENDS ON EARTH	- Sanjay Kant	Rs. 75
30. GOOD CHANCES (2nd Reprint)	- Howard Levin	Rs. 120
31. HEART TO HEART (2st Reprint)	- Howard Levin	Rs. 120
32. HOLY MISSION DIVINE VISION	- Sai Usha	Rs. 80
33. IN QUEST OF GOD	- P. P. Arya	Rs. 120
34. JOURNEY OF GRACE	- Cynthia Harris	Rs. 140
35. KNOW THYSELF (2nd Revised Ed.)	- Gerard T. Satvic	Rs. 200
36. LET ME SOW LOVE	- Doris May Gibson	Rs. 120
37. LETTERS FROM A GRANDFATHER	- S. K. Bose	Rs. 180
38. MESSAGES (Japanese)	- Dr. M. N. Rao	Rs. 150
39. MESSAGES FROM MY DEAREST FRIEND SAI BABA	- Elvie Bailey	Rs. 130

40. MIRACLES ARE MY VISITING CARDS	- Erlendur Haraldsson	Rs. 180
41. MOHANA BALA SAI (Children's Book)	- Sai Mira	Rs. 120
42. MUKTI THE LION FINDS HIMSELF	- Gina Suritsch	Rs. 85
43. ONENESS OF DIVINITY	- Ratan Lal	Rs. 100
44. PATH OF THE PILGRIM	- Richard Selby	Rs. 120
45. PRASANTHI GUIDE (Revised Ed.)	- R. Padmanaban	Rs. 100
46. SAI BABA AND NARA NARAYANA GUFA ASHRAM Part III	- Swami Maheswaranand	Rs. 30
47. SAI BABA GITA	- Al Drucker	Rs. 200
48. SAI BABA'S SONG BIRD	- Lightstorm	Rs. 60
49. SAI BABA: THE ETERNAL COMPANION	- B. P. Misra	Rs. 200
50. SAI HUMOUR	- Peggy Mason, et. all.	Rs. 70
51. SAI NAAMAAVALI	- Jagat Narain Tripathi	Rs. 90
52. SATHYA SAI'S AMRITA VARSHINI	- Sudha Aditya	Rs. 75
53. SATHYA SAI'S ANUGRAHA VARSHINI	- Sudha Aditya	Rs. 90
54. SAI SANDESH	- Sai Usha	Rs. 50
55. SAI'S STORY	- Shaila Hattiangadi	Rs. 75
56. SATVIC FOOD & HEALTH (2nd Revised Ed.)	- Gerard T. Satvic	Rs. 45
57. SATVIC STORIES	- Benjamin Kurzweil	Rs. 40
58. SELF REALISATION	- Al Drucker	Rs. 50
59. SPIRITUAL IMPRESSIONS A Bi-monthly Magazine	- Sai Towers	Rs. 100
60. SPRINKLES OF GOLDEN DUST	- Jeannette Caruth	Rs. 65
61. SRI SATHYA SAI BABA AND WONDERS OF HIS LOVE	- John Elliott	Rs. 90
62. SRI SATHYA SAI CHALEESA	- B. P. Mishra	Rs. 15
63. SRI SATHYA SAI BABA PRAYER BOOK	- Sai Towers	Rs. 10
64. SRI SATHYA SAI BABA YOUNG ADULTS PROGRAMME	- L. A. Ramdath	Rs. 80
65. STUDY CIRCLES FOR DIVINITY	- Ross Woodward & Ron Farmer	Rs. 390
66. TEN STEPS TO KESAVA	- Lightstorm	Rs. 150
67. THE ARMOUR OF SRI SATHYA SAI	- O. P. Vidyakar	Rs. 10
68. THE DIVINE LEELAS OF BHAGAVAN SRI SATHYA SAI BABA	- Nagamani Purnaiya	Rs. 100
69. THE GRACE OF SAI	- R. Lowenberg	Rs. 120
70. THE HEART OF SAI	- R. Lowenberg	Rs. 130
71. THE OMNIPRESENCE OF SAI	- R. Lowenberg	Rs. 120
72. THE PHOENIX RETURNS	- Kristina Gale-Kumar	Rs. 250
73. THE PROPHECY	- Barbara Gardner	Rs. 120
74. THE SCRIPTURES ARE FULFILLED	- Kristina Gale-Kumar	Rs. 160
75. THE THOUSAND SONGS OF LORD VISHNU	- Jeannette Caruth	Rs. 150
76. THY WILL BE DONE	- C. D. Mirchandani	Rs. 90
77. TOWARDS A BETTER LIFE- Word Images from Sai Teachings (10 cards)		Rs. 50
78. WAITING FOR BABA	- V. Ramnath	Rs. 95
79. WHO IS BABA?	- Margaret Tottle-Smith	Rs. 60
80. YOU ARE GOD	- M. N. Rao	Rs. 150
81. YOUR LIFE IS YOUR MESSAGE	- Charlene Leslie Chaden	Rs. 225

FORTHCOMING PUBLICATIONS ...

01 A COMPENDIUM OF SAI BHAJANS — R. Padmanaban
02 DIRECTORY OF MASTERS, SAINTS
    AND ASHRAMS IN INDIA — R. Padmanaban
03. FOUNTAIN OF LOVE
    An Overview of Sathya Sai Water Supply Project — R. Padmanaban
04. KRISHNAMURTHI AND THE FOURTH WAY — Evan Gram
05. LOVE IS MY FORM VOL. I The Advent
    Pictorial Biography of Sri Sathya Sai Baba — R. Padmanaban
06. ONE SOUL'S JOURNEY — Leni Matlin
07. VOICE OF THE AVATAR — Compilation of Yearwise Volumes of Discourses of Bhagawan Sri Sathya Sai Baba

OUR DISTRIBUTORS

Australia
Mr. James Somers
13 Hunter Street, Parramatta NSW 2150
Phone   : (02) 9687 2441
Fax   : (02) 9687 2449

Canada
Sri Sathya Sai Books & Information Centre
290 Merton Street, Toranto
Ontario M 4S 1 A9
Phone   : (416) 481 7342
Fax   : (416) 498 0270 / 345 9212
E-mail: saibooks@idirect.ca

England
Sai Books UK Limited
21, Greystone Gardens
Harrow Middlex, HA3 0EF
Phone   : (181) 907 1267
Fax   : (181) 909 3954
E-mail: saibooks@btinternet.com

India
Sai Towers Brindavan
23/1142 Vijayalakshmi Colony
Kadugodi, Bangalore 560 067
Phone   : (080) 8451648
Fax: : (080) 8451649

Europe (excluding England)
Sathya Sai Book Shop
Laurenzenvorstadt 87
CH - 5000 AARAU Switzerland
Tel / Fax: (62) 822 3722
E-mail : 13042.2123 @compuserve.com

Malaysia
Sathya Sai Baba Centre of Bangsar
24, Jalan Abdullah, off Jalan Bangsar
59000 Kuala Lumpur
Phone   : (3) 254 5224 / 241 3646

New Zealand
Sathya Sai Publications
P.O. Box 56-347 Dominion Road
Auckland 1003
Phone   : (9) 638 8210
Fax   : (9) 638 8159
E-mail : ravi@titan.co.nz

Singapore
P. Ramanathan
Block 1M, Pine Grove No. 01- 43
Singapore 591201   Phone : 466 5983

West Indies
Ace Printery Fed Traders Ltd.
34-36, Pasea Main Road
Tunapuna, Trinidad & Tobago
Phone/Fax : (868) 663 (2273)
663 2152, 3223
E-mail :ramdhan@ carib-link.ne

U.S.A.
Jai Sai Ram
PO Box 900 Trinidad,
CO 81082 U.S.A.
Phone   : (719) 846 0846
Fax   : (719) 846 0847
E-Mail : jaisairm @ ria.net (or)
         jaisairm @ rmi.net